Footprints of the Soul

A Creative Guide
For Spiritual Journey Groups and Individuals

Permissions

Grateful acknowledgment is made for permission to reproduce the following material: Reprinted by permission of HarperCollins Publishers Inc. "Matins I & II" from *Eternal Echoes: Exploring Our Yearning To Belong* by John O'Donohue, copyright 1999 by John O'Donohue. Submitted excerpt fr. p. 6 from *Will and Spirit* by Gerald G. May, copyright 1983 by Gerald G. May. Submitted excerpt fr. p.50 from *Plain and Simple: A Woman's Journey to the Amish* by Sue Bender, copyright 1991 by Sue Bender. "A Friendship Blessing" from *Anam Cara: A Book of Celtic Wisdom* by John O'Donohue, copyright 1997 by John O'Donohue. Submitted excerpt fr. p.28 from *Awakening the Heroes Within* by Carol S. Pearson, copyright 1991 by Carol S.Pearson. Submitted excerpt from *Care of Mind/Care of Spirit* by Gerald G. May, copyright 1982 by Gerald G. May. Submitted excerpt fr. p.24 from *Study Guide for Celebration of Discipline* by Richard J. Foster, copyright 1983 by Richard J. Foster. Reprinted with permission from *Embrace Tiger Return to Mountain* by Chungliang Al Huang, copyright 1997 by Chungliang Al Huang, Celestial Arts, Berkeley, CA. Reprinted by permission of New Directions Publishing Corp. a 40 word excerpt from *Siddhartha* by Herman Hess, copyright 1951 by New Directions Publishing Corp. Used with permission of Paulist Press excerpts from *God and You* by William Barry, copyright 1987 by Paulist Press, Inc., *Listening For the Heartbeat of God* by Philip Newell, copyright 1997 by Paulist Press, Inc., *Understanding Christian Spirituality* by Michael Downey, copyright 1997 by Paulist Press, Inc. Reprinted by permission of Wood Lake Books an excerpt from *Healing from the Heart* by Graham, Litt & Irwin, p.21, copyright 1998 by Wood Lake Books. Reprinted by permission of Riverhead Books, an imprint of Penguin Putnam, Inc. an excerpt from *Walking a Sacred Path* by Lauren Artress, copyright 1995 by Lauren Artress. Used by permission of Jeremy P. Tarcher,an imprint of Penguin Group (USA) Inc.an excerpt from *Creativity: Where the Divine and the Human Meet* by Matthew Fox, copyright 2002 by Matthew Fox. Used by permission of Westminster John Knox Press excerpts from *A Book of Reformed Prayer* by Howard Rice, *Healing Touch: The Churches Forgotten Language* by Zach Thomas, *Soul Feast* by Marjorie Thompson, and *Primary Speech* by Ann and Barry Ulanov. Used by permission of Random House-Bertelsmann excerpts from *Ordinary Graces* by Lorraine Kisly, *Aha!* by Jordan Ayan, and *Ageless Body, Timeless Mind* by Deepak Chopra. Used by permission of University of California Press an excerpt from *After Heaven: Spirituality in America Since the 1950's* by Robert Wuthnow, copyright 1998 by the Regents of the University of California. Used by permission from Beacon Press an excerpt from *The Healing Connection* by Jean Baker Miller and Irene Stiver, copyright 1997 by Beacon Press. Used by permission of Morehouse Publishing an excerpt from *Still Listening* by Norvene Vest, copyright 2000 by Norvene Vest. Used by permission of John Wiley & Sons, Inc. an excerpt from *Let Your Life Speak* by Parker Palmer, copyright 2000. Used by permission from the authors excerpts from *Swallow's Nest* by Marchiene Rienstra, copyright 1992, *Called into Healing* by Linda Smith, copyright 2000, *Life Is Change – Growth Is Optional* by Karen Kaiser Clark, copyright 1993 and *Celtic Meditations* by Edward J. Farrell, copyright 1976.

The scripture quotations contained herein are from The Spiritual Formation Bible, New Revised Standard Version, copyrighted by The Zondervan Corporation, 1999.

Cover design by Christine Collins Woomer

The cover art represents the soul's journey into the joyous celebration of the fullness of abundant life. This spiritual journey is supported by a bridge honoring all the cycles of life and nature, and is purified and sustained by Divine water.

In Memory of a True Soul Friend,

Tom Pantlind

Acknowledgments

I wish to express the deepest gratitude to all of the following people, who have helped to make this book possible:

Sue Azzar, Jen Azzar, Sonja M. Stewart Ph.D., The Rev. Jean Attwood Miller, The Rev. Dr. Robert K. Livingston, Nancy Romant, Donna Rathert, M.R.E., Chris Woomer, Julie Metsker, Beth Code, The Rev. Kevin E Holley, Dan Pierson, my family and friends, and all the members of the initial spirituality group.

Table of Contents

Preface

Footprints of the Soul has emerged out of a series of gatherings that I have led for a group of people seeking to deepen their connection to the Divine. The group members came from diverse religious backgrounds, some attending places of worship, others not. Most of them did not previously know each other. The members' comments about their experiences in the group spiritual journey process are included at the back of the book. As a spiritual director and secondary school teacher, I relished the opportunity not only to help create sacred space and time for them, but also to participate myself in the rich shared experience. As God's spirit moved among us, we each found a renewed self, one focused on the centrality of Divine love, peace and guidance in our lives.

My intention was to offer exposure to a wide variety of contemplative prayer forms from Christian and other faith traditions so that participants could create their own meaningful spiritual practice. Many of them did expand their private devotional time, but I discovered that the most profound learning and change happened within the context of the group. Sandra Lomasson describes this in the article "Tending the Communal Soul in a Congregational Setting." "There was a communal soul being revealed with its particular dimensions, as well as a distinct charism and call, and this soul was more than the aggregate of individual souls." (Vest, Norvene. Still Listening, p. 137) Through participating in the Footprints of the Soul spiritual journey process, participants have formed a group soul that tends us all, whether we are together or apart.

I have been profoundly blessed by this group of people who encouraged me to write this guide so that others could form spiritual journey groups. My vision is that it be used by groups of diverse men and women of all ages, thereby adding a deeper dimension to understandings of faith among humankind.

As part of my training in spiritual direction, I was asked to research a particular religious tradition to present to the class. Because of my Scottish heritage, I chose the Celtic Christian Church. I fell in love with this beautiful spirituality and was fortunate to spend a week at a retreat on Lake Tahoe led by Howard Rice from the San Francisco Theological Seminary. The retreat, "Celtic Spirituality: Recovering Our Spiritual Roots," solidified this tradition as my foundation in faith. I have incorporated many aspects of Celtic spirituality into the fifteen "Journeys" or units of prayer that comprise my process for a creative approach to prayer. While Christianity is the foundation of this guidebook, I have also woven in material that represents a diverse spiritual perspective.

What follows has come out of my education in spiritual direction, combined with my experience in working with individuals and groups as an educator. I am grateful for the willingness of these people to participate in this sacred work and for their support in the compilation of the book.

It is my hope that this guide will richly bless the lives of all who decide to embark on the search for more spiritual meaning and guidance for their lives. May God be with us as we journey together.

Blessings on the Journey,
Elizabeth Wood Willey
June 10, 2002
Grand Rapids, Michigan

My Vision for Spiritual Journeys

In writing this guidebook, <u>Footprints of the Soul</u>, it is my vision to create a process that can be used in a variety of ways and settings to assist individuals and groups in deepening their connection to the Divine. Through experiencing a wide variety of prayer forms, an expanded understanding of God and spiritual practice is developed. It is my belief that when persons participate in such a process, a sacred community is formed where God is present in a profound way, offering safety, solace, and a deeper sense of self. Some of the suggested arenas where this guidebook would be effective are:

1. Churches that wish to offer the opportunity for ongoing spiritual formation to their congregations.

2. Ministry groups that wish to deepen a healing presence, such as Parish Nurses or Stephen Ministry.

3. High school youth groups within a church or a school open to offering spiritual formation.

4. Using one or more of the Journeys as part of an adult educational series.

5. Individuals who wish to use the material independently.

6. Families wishing to share a spiritual journey together.

7. Spiritual direction in a group setting inclusive of different religious backgrounds.

8. Groups that wish to gather outside an established church or religious setting to share ideas and experiences.

9. Retirement or nursing homes.

10. Staff members in organizations open to building spiritual community.

In <u>Footprints of the Soul</u> there are 15 "Journeys," or units of prayer. A Journey represents the suggested theme, prayer forms, and supporting material for each group gathering. Because each one of the Journeys presented is autonomous, it also can be used separately by individuals for private prayer time.

The first five Journeys, or units of prayer, are foundational. They are used to build an understanding of the many forms of prayer and to establish familiarity with the methodology I present. Learning to listen prayerfully to the experience of others is also foundational to the material. A daylong retreat follows these five units to share life stories. Sharing life stories within a spiritual context is a key component in the forming of sacred community, building familiarity, and trust. The remaining ten Journeys are thematic and can be used in any order. This gives the group the opportunity to choose what they would like to share at the next gathering. For example, the Journey on "Gratitude" could be used around Thanksgiving.

A Format for Each Journey

Gathering

a. An opening time of silence and centering.

b. The opportunity for participants to share briefly how they are coming to the gathering. Other than the first two gatherings, which have an introductory focus, two questions are suggested for the remaining gatherings:

How are you in mind/body/spirit?

What has been your experience of the Divine since we last gathered?

Presenting the Theme

A variety of readings and quotes related to the theme are read out loud by group members. These are not meant to open up a lengthy discussion but to offer, instead, a variety of viewpoints and to focus attention on the given theme.

Prayer

a. An experience of prayer often followed by journaling and drawing.

b. An opportunity for participants to share what they felt or learned during the prayer time. This is a time of "holy" listening, or being present to each other in an open, non-judgmental way.

c. Some of the units include a form of moving prayer to embody the given theme.

Closing

Closing with a blessing or reading.

Journal Pages

At the end of each Journey there is space to journal and draw. After a prayer experience it is beneficial to first journal and then draw images or pictures that represent one's personal experience. These activities support the awareness that considering it in a variety of ways deepens a time of prayer. The space also can be used for journaling between gatherings. Participants can then refer back to their previous spiritual experience. This can be very helpful in seeing personal change or in reinforcing their commitment to a God-centered life.

Guided Meditations

"The soul never speaks without a picture." *Aristotle*

In many of the Journeys, guided meditations are suggested. A CD is included so no member of the group has to read a meditation, therefore missing the opportunity to participate in this important creative process. The use of the imagination, as well as the rational mind, is key to grasping what lies beyond human understanding. Through guided meditation, the imagination provides images for our soul's expression.

"Imagination is a gift of God, and in ancient Christian theology it was referred to as the thought of the heart." (Oldfield, David. 1987)

Individual Use of <u>Footprints of the Soul</u>

Individuals can effectively use <u>Footprints of the Soul</u> by creating a sacred space, following the format presented in each Journey, listening to the guided meditations, and journaling at the end of each prayer experience. Also, if an individual who is part of a group cannot attend a gathering, he or she can do a missed journey on their own and then be ready to move on with their group.

Footprints of the Soul

There is a deep hunger for experiencing a sense of connection or oneness with a Divine Source. In <u>After Heaven: Spirituality in America Since 1950</u>, Robert Wuthnow, a sociology professor at Princeton, writes that the traditional spirituality of inhabiting a sacred space has given way to a new spirituality of seeking.

Now at the end of the 20th century, growing numbers of Americans piece together their faith like a patchwork quilt. Spirituality has become a vastly complex quest in which each person seeks in his or her own way. In my view, the ancient wisdom that emphasizes the idea of spiritual practices needs to be rediscovered. Though spiritual practices can and do take many different forms, their common denominator is a commitment to engaging intentionally in activities that deepen one's relationship to the sacred. Characteristics of spiritual practice typically include discernment; a new vision of self; a sharing of experiences and stories with others; emphasis upon an ethical dimension; and the use of a wide variety of resources for inner work: meditation, contemplative prayer, chanting, dancing and other forms of stylized movement, devotional reading; service to others; to name only a few. (<u>Ions</u>, Aug.-Nov., 1999)

Mystics of all the world religious traditions knew that in order to directly experience the presence of God, there must be a shift in consciousness through quieting the mind and body and going within to find stillness and peace. Various ancient forms of contemplative prayer have been adapted for contemporary use and are being widely used in adult groups, as well as in high school youth groups, and in churches of diverse denominations.

As a spiritual director I know how important it is to encourage people to find times of solitude, but I also believe it is necessary to share and discover with others the purpose and meaning of life. <u>Footprints of the Soul</u> groups offer the opportunity to experience a wide range of being with Divine presence and to participate in group dialogue focused on sharing insights from participants' faith journeys. This is primarily a time of listening and honoring each person's unique experience rather than a discussion or problem solving exercise.

<u>Footprints of the Soul</u> is my vision of combining my experiences as a high school teacher and a spiritual director. I hope to help people of all ages learn to listen to the guidance of their soul by discovering and developing their own spiritual practices. As an educator, I believe that each individual's experience is so unique that it is helpful to apply Howard Gardner's theory of multiple intelligence to one's spiritual life. Gardner, a professor at Harvard's Graduate School of Education in 1983, described eight styles of learning and stated that each person is born with a unique combination of strengths and weaknesses in these styles. However, he believed that all of them could be more fully developed in an individual through experience. As I describe each learning style, I offer suggestions of various forms of prayer that will support each one. Individuals will naturally be drawn to one or two styles and can begin to create their spiritual practice from a place of comfort. They will also have the opportunity to grow through other prayer forms. Hopefully, each individual will feel enriched by the shared stories and learn new ways of being with God.

Prayer Forms for Eight Learning Styles

1. Linguistic – writing, reading, speaking

   a. Journaling
   b. Lectio Divina (a sacred meditation with scripture)
   c. Sharing faith stories with others

2. Logical/Mathematical – reasoning, exploring patterns

   a. Life mapping
   b. Reading sacred scriptures

3. Spatial – visualizing, sensing, working with color

   a. Dream analysis
   b. Artwork expressing spirituality
   c. Guided imagery

4. Musical – rhythm, melody, composing

   a. Meditating with music
   b. Singing
   c. Drumming

5. Bodily/kinesthetic – touching, moving

   a. Liturgical dance
   b. Tai Chi/Yoga
   c. Walking the Labyrinth
   d. Focusing Prayer

6. Interpersonal – relating, sharing with others

   a. Group spiritual direction
   b. Group retreats

7. Intrapersonal – understanding self, working alone

   a. Centering Prayer
   b. Individual guided retreat

8. Natural World – learning through immersion in nature

   a. Wilderness trips with focus on spirituality
   b. Praying through nature
   c. Walking prayer

Spiritual Journey as Spiritual Formation

Embarking upon a spiritual journey is a commitment to opening oneself to be recreated or formed by God as one lives from day to day. It is a dynamic process that is circular, ever widening and deepening. Marjorie J. Thompson describes spiritual formation in this way:

"God's Spirit is continually challenging, changing and maturing us. Although we may be able to point to a single and decisive conversion experience, remaining faithful involves a journey of continual conversion. Spiritual growth is a work of divine grace with which we are called to cooperate. Opening ourselves to the work of the spirit requires effort and discipline." _Soul Feast_, p. 8

This guidebook, Footprints of the Soul, is my image of the beginning and ongoing movement of this life-giving spiritual formation process. The beginning focus is on past footprints, looking behind at where we have walked in life, remembering if and when we have felt Divine presence. Life stories are shared visually through a process called life mapping so that the group can share in honoring the sacred life experiences of each member. In his book, Care of the Soul, Thomas Moore says, "Soul is not a thing, but a quality or a dimension of experiencing life and ourselves. It has to do with depth, value, relatedness, heart, and personal substance." (Care of the Soul, p. 5) Believing that each person's soul is unique, I offer a process that will present a wide variety of experiences to deepen inner awareness and sense of connection to the Divine.

To move forward on a spiritual journey, we are called to listen carefully to where our inner guidance is calling us to go and to watch for the emerging footprints leading to our original wholeness and God's unique purpose for our lives. A spiritual journey group forms a sacred community where we may share in the celebration of the mystery and beauty of each life. The experience offers time for individual reflection and time to listen to and learn from each other, fostering both self-compassion and a sense of connection to soul friends.

The journey includes the challenge of sorting through belief systems, relationship issues, old wounds, and other blocks that keep us from embracing God's love and grace. As these challenges are recognized and released in creative and prayerful ways, our spirit is free to grow in joy and creativity. The authentic self begins to emerge with more courage and strength to co-create life with God. Our inner experience becomes more connected to the lived reality as we seek to align belief and action within the context of our faith.

A spiritual pathway often begins within the context of the beliefs and rituals of a particular religious tradition, but this can move from belief to knowing, through direct and personal experience. It calls for the honoring of others' experiences, even though their pathways may be different. An alive spirituality is the capacity of the human spirit to receive, reflect, and respond to the spirit of God. It involves a conscious awareness of choices of belief, value commitments, patterns of life, and practices of faith that allow people to fully realize their spiritual potential. Learning to listen in silence, we can allow the mystery of life to unfold as we are guided by an indwelling spirit. This activity draws us to something larger than ourselves, so that our faith is alive through connecting to other souls and taking action in the world. Integrating transcendent mystery into our daily lives leads to both transformation and freedom. As we each cultivate a personal relationship with God as a source of strength and vision, we place ourselves where we can receive God's blessings and participate in the transformation of our soul.

John 4:14

Those who drink of the water that I will give them will never be thirsty.
The water that I will give will become in them
a spring of water gushing up to eternal life.

Two Formation Models for the Spiritual Journey

There are two formation models that I believe are important to consider when entering into a spiritual journey process. Ideas from both models are woven into the material. The first was developed by Adrian van Kamm, the founder of Duquesne University's Institute of Formative Spirituality. Formative Spirituality approaches human growth from all levels: the spiritual, mental, physical, and social. It considers how all aspects of one's being can integrate to give support and insight into living everyday life. The dimensions that must be balanced are socio-historic, vital, functional, and transcendent. The socio-historic dimension looks at the beliefs, perspectives and traditions that influence an individual's life. The vital dimension refers to the physical aspect of an individual, while the functional considers how one organizes and reacts to life. Most important is the transcendent dimension, focused on living life open to God. VanKaam believes that it should guide the other dimensions. Not only does he encourage a holistic approach to formation, but also he states that each individual has a formation field that is unique. It is composed of one's own life situation, relationships with self and others, the culture, and the world. Key to his thesis is that one is continually being formed by this field and also is active in forming it.

Taking into account these emphases by Van Kamm, a group formation process offers the opportunity for us to become conscious of how these important aspects integrate personally with a life centered on God. We develop a more balanced approach to our spirituality and become more aware of how we can co-create our lives in partnership with the Divine. *Presence: The Journal of Spiritual Directors International*, Volume 7: no. 1 – 2

The second model was offered by Teilhard de Chardin, theologian and paleontologist, who spoke of three interconnected and dynamic tasks that are part of a mature spiritual formation. The first task is to develop ourselves, fostering self-knowledge and integration. The second is to extend ourselves compassionately to others, forgiving unconditionally, and choosing for the common good. Finally, we are called to open ourselves to be formed by the working of the Spirit within, surrendering to the will of God in our lives. *Surrender*, pp. 133 & 134

As participants experience the Journeys and Retreat in <u>Footprints of the Soul</u>, they will be given the opportunity to open to how all aspects of their lives are rooted in the presence of God. New ways of being with the fullness of their own personal journeys will lead to an integration of body, mind, and spirit. They will be encouraged to grow in relationship to God and to move from that connection, to relating to others and the world with a deep sense of compassion.

Fruits of Spiritual Practice on the Spiritual Journey

The formation process encourages the development of meaningful spiritual practices. If we are faithful to this, there are many fruits to be gathered, thereby enriching life by:

1. Learning to draw from inner spirit for self-renewal.

2. Experiencing the sacredness of everyday life.

3. Bringing ourselves into balance, integrating mind, body, emotions, and spirit.

4. Living in celebration, wonder, and gratitude.

5. Viewing life as continually being created.

6. Developing a sense of sacred time or kairos time.

7. Cultivating I-Thou relationships, seeing others as carriers of the Divine.

8. Participating in inclusive communities that value diversity.

9. Liberating and cultivating the human spirit in self and others.

10. Developing love and compassion for self and others.

11. Bringing faith and hope alive in the world through work and service.

"By themselves the Spiritual Disciplines can do nothing; they only get us to the place where something can be done... the means by which we place ourselves where God can bless us." *Richard Foster, Quaker pastor*

Forming the Spirituality Group

When beginning to gather a group of people who desire to deepen their spiritual experience, it is best to give a brief description of the process, as well as some guidelines for individuals to consider before committing to joining the group. I sent out the following information to anyone who inquired about the group:

1. The group consists of 8 – 12 people committed to attending gatherings.

2. The experience includes the use of a variety of prayer forms such as contemplative Christian prayer, moving prayer (such as walking the labyrinth), prayer through creative methods, and ways of praying with other faith traditions.

3. Each gathering begins with the sharing of experiences of faith that may have occurred since the previous group. We then participate in a new prayer form, followed by a period of silence. Individuals have the opportunity to comment on their personal insights or feelings if they choose to do so. This is primarily a time of listening to and honoring each person's unique experience rather than a discussion or problem-solving exercise.

4. The purpose of the group is to grow the individual's sense of creating a life in cooperation with God by offering a wide range of experiences that can help each person develop meaningful spiritual practices.

5. Another important focus is to form a sacred community that shares the common vision of deepening a journey with the Divine. A retreat follows Journey 5 to facilitate this.

6. Confidentiality is essential and must be honored.

7. The group gathers every two to three weeks on an agreed upon day, with each meeting lasting about one and one–half hours.

Creating Sacred Space

The process of creating a sacred space is key to bringing a contemplative experience to the minds and hearts of the participants. Without it, the group can tend to turn to discussion or problem solving without a focus on the interior movement of God in each person. It is best to find a quiet, private space to meet where the group can gather in a circle around a small table. There also should be room for individuals to spread out for private meditation, journaling, drawing, or movement. Our group met in a church that graciously let us use a room, and there was usually a ping pong tournament going on above us. It was amazing how quickly we adapted to the noise!

I suggest that a small table be placed in the center of the circle to serve as an altar, with the content changing from week to week. Our altar always had a cloth, a candle, a Christian cross, something from the natural world, and something representing other religious traditions. Group members were encouraged to bring something sacred to them or pictures for special prayer requests. One of the group members always brought a prayer shawl that was a gift from a Tibetan Buddhist monk who once was her houseguest. I brought my Tibetan Harmony Bowl to use as a beginning and ending to prayer time or guided meditation.

At the beginning of our gathering, we would light the candle (symbolic of Divine presence), and sit quietly for a few minutes to center ourselves and deepen our awareness of God's presence among us. Participants would then share with the group how they were in mind/body/spirit, using a word or phrase for each. They also shared what had been an experience of God for them since we last met. (20 minutes)

Next, we would take turns reading scripture or other materials pertaining to the theme for the gathering. This would focus our minds and hearts on the topic. There might be some comment or explanation, but lengthy discussion was discouraged so that more time could be spent on the experiential segment. (10 minutes)

The prayer experience varied. It included contemplative prayer, guided meditation, journaling, drawing, moving, or a combination of these. It became important to leave time, usually one half hour, for group members to share their experiences. This was a time of honoring and listening. Group members were encouraged to reflect on how they had been impacted by the experiences of the others, without giving advice or judgment. (50 minutes)

After Journey 5 and the Retreat, the group can mutually agree on the theme for the next gathering and decide who will lead it. At this point, the Journeys do not have to be guided by the leader who was trained to use the book. Other group members should be encouraged to take a leadership role. Then one member would close by offering the suggested blessing or reading. (10 minutes)

Five Foundational Journeys

The first five Journeys in <u>Footprints of the Soul</u> are foundational because they teach key elements of this spiritual journey process. They should be experienced in order and prior to the retreat. The following concepts are necessary for participants to have a successful experience:

1. An understanding of different forms of prayer and how they relate to individual learning styles. (Journeys 1 & 2)

2. A focus on how to be a "soul friend" or non-judgmental listener with a loving presence. (Journey 3)

3. The awareness that the presence of the Divine is woven into the fabric of their daily lives. (Journey 4)

4. The opportunity to reflect on their life stories within a spiritual context. The element of trust and a deeper understanding of each other are developed through the sharing of life maps. (Journey 5)

5. The opportunity to experience and learn the particular order and process included in each Journey.

A Retreat

A day-long retreat follows Journey 5. It should be scheduled at the first gathering. The retreat serves to solidify a sense of community and offers enough time to share life maps. Offering the retreat at a location with access to the natural world is a wonderful addition because it gives individuals the opportunity to do some meditation with nature.

Journeys 6 – 15

These Journeys are thematic and can be used in any order the group chooses. Group members are encouraged to lead these journeys.

Leader Formation

A daylong Leader's Workshop will be offered for individuals who wish to learn how to use these materials effectively. I do not believe that persons need to be ordained clergy, trained spiritual directors, or teachers to be able to help form a spiritual journey group. Through experiencing the materials in a Leader's Workshop, individuals will be able to take <u>Footprints of the Soul</u> and guide a group in their chosen setting.

It is best if the foundational journeys are led by an individual who has gone through a day-long training that offers the opportunity to experience and learn the <u>Footprints</u> process. After the retreat, leadership of the group may be rotated among other members of the group. Information about Leader Workshops can be found on the web site www.footprintsofthesoul.com.

Materials Needed

The materials needed for all of the sessions are a <u>Footprints of the Soul</u> guidebook for each participant, markers, pens, pencils, and extra paper. The guided meditation CD is included in the pocket at the back of the book.

Additionally, the CDs with the music for each gathering and a CD player are required. The recommended CDs are listed with each Journey and also in the reference section at the back of the book.

Gathering

1. Welcome everyone and ask that name tags be worn for this first session. Allow enough time for everyone to introduce themselves with a little information and to talk about why they have joined the group. They could also mention what their spiritual practices, if any, might be at this point.

2. Light the candle and ask for a few moments of silence to center individually and as a group. Play Guided Meditation #1, using the CD in the back of the book to teach slow rhythmic breathing with attention on the breath.

3. Explain about sacred space and invite group members to bring personal items for the altar placed at the center of the circle. They may bring items that represent their connection to the Divine or prayer concerns.

Presenting the Theme

1. Review the concept of prayer related to multiple learning styles and discuss the importance of listening to each other without judging or giving advice. Be sure to emphasize confidentiality.

2. Take turns reading the selections on prayer. (see p. 2)

Prayer

1. Play Guided Meditation # 2, "God in my Breath," adapted from Sadhana, p. 36.

2. After a period of 5 – 10 minutes of silence, bring attention back to the group and offer participants the opportunity to comment on their experience. (see p. 3)

3. Present the concept of the "Sacred Segmenting of the Day." Before the beginning of each day, they consider all the different aspects of it. Then they may choose to stop before each part of the day to bless it or ask for help and guidance. (see p. 3)

4. Encourage everyone to begin to set aside a period of time each day to be quiet and allow themselves to "rest in Divine love."

Closing

1. Read "A Celtic Blessing." (see p. 4)

References
Barry, William. God And You. New Jersey: Paulist Press, 1987.
de Mello, Anthony. Sadhana, A Way to God. New York: Doubleday, 1984.
Foster, Richard. Celebration of Discipline Study Guide. San Francisco: HarperCollins, 1983.
Nouwen, Henry. With Open Hands. Notre Dame, IN: Ave Maria Press, 1995.
Ulanov, Ann & Barry. Primary Speech. Atlanta: John Knox Press, 1982.

Prayer

"A word about getting out of your head: The head is not a very good place for prayer. It is not a bad place for starting your prayer. But if your prayer stays there too long and doesn't move into the heart, it will gradually dry up and prove tiresome and frustrating. You must learn to move out of the area of thinking and talking and move into the area of feeling, sensing, loving and intuiting. That is the area where contemplation is born and prayer becomes a transforming power and a source of never-ending delight and peace." *de Mello, Anthony. Sadhana, p. 17*

"The first misconception is the notion that prayer mainly involves asking things from God. Answers to prayer are wonderful, but they are secondary to the main function of prayer, which is a growing perpetual communion…to discover God in all of the moments of our days, and to be pleased rather than perturbed at the discovery – this is the stuff of prayer. It is out of this refreshing life of communion that answered prayer comes as a happy by-product." *Foster, Richard. Study Guide for Celebration of Discipline, p. 24*

"If we go on listening, we feel God pulling us, drawing us into another current, a larger, deeper, stronger one than our usual little force. Prayer tugs at us, pulls us into a life of abundance, of unceasing abundance. We become increasingly swept into the flowing of this other life through the small space of our self. Prayer takes us into our central self, and through it into the very origin of all self. The speech of prayer tells us of the new life for psyche and soul that comes when we open the door to the one who stands there knocking." *Ulanov, Ann and Barry. Primary Speech, p. 9*

"Unawareness of the God who is so intimately in relationship with us may show itself in occasional anxiety about the meaning of life, or in a frantic search for answers to life's mystery, or in overwork or overindulgence of some kind. Knowing who we are – in our depths – is salutary and freeing even if a bit daunting. So God does want us to be in conscious relationship with him. And conscious relationship is prayer, another way of saying that prayer is the raising of the mind and heart to God." *Barry, William. God and You, p. 12, 13*

"And yet, compassion is possible when it has roots in prayer. For in prayer you do not depend on your own strength, nor on the good will of another, but only on your trust in God. That is why prayer makes you free to live a compassionate life even when it does not evoke a grateful response or bring immediate rewards."
Nouwen, Henry. With Open Hands, p. 33

Suggested questions for processing the prayer experience as a group:

1. What was that like for you?

2. Were you able to let go and experience a sense of being with the meditation?

3. What did you notice in your body?

4. What feelings did you experience?

5. Did any images come up for you?

6. Were you able to stop mind chatter?

7. Do you feel different after the experience?

8. How might you use this?

These questions are meant to apply to all the Journey experiences. Not all of them need to be asked, but they are meant to give the leader ideas for how to lead the group sharing segment. It is important to trust what comes to mind without analyzing. This is more of an intuitive experience. After the first few Journeys, group members will become more comfortable with the processing and sharing of their prayer experience.

Sacred Segmenting of the Day

1. Spend a few minutes first thing in the morning considering all the aspects of the coming day.

2. Image each segment of the day, and ask for blessings, peace, and guidance.

3. As you move into each new segment, take the time to be quiet, breath deeply, and become centered so that you will be totally present to what is happening. Be aware that Divine presence is with you in all that you do.

4. At the end of the day, spend quiet time recalling each segment. Consider how God may have been present to you.

5. Give thanks for all the experiences of your life.

A Celtic Blessing

May the road rise to meet you.

May a wind always be at your back.

May the sunshine be warm upon your face.

May the rain fall soft upon your field.

Until we meet again.

May God hold you in the palm of His hand.

May the Lord bless you and keep you and

May the Lord cause His face to shine upon you

And give you peace.

Amen

Guided Meditation #1

Learning deep rhythmic breathing is key to entering into meditation. I will first explain the process and then guide you through the experience. First listen to these instructions:

Breathe deeply and rhythmically to the count of four. Fill your belly on the first count, your solar plexus (mid-body) on the second count, your heart on the third count, and your throat on the fourth count. Hold for one count. Release the breath starting at the throat, then the heart, the solar plexus, and finally the belly. Hold for one count. I will count two full breaths for you and then you complete three more full breaths on your own. Follow your breath with your mind, making the in-breath equal to the out-breath. As you breathe in, image the light of God filling every cell of your body with nurturing and healing. As you release the breath, image sending peace out into the world.
Beginning the breathing now, inhale with the count of four, imaging the light of God pouring into all the cells of your body, 1 – 2 – 3 – 4, hold. Exhale peace, 1 – 2 – 3 – 4, hold. Again, inhale, 1 – 2 – 3 – 4. Exhale-1 – 2 – 3 – 4.

Allow the sound of the Tibetan Harmony Bowl to draw you more deeply into the sanctuary at the center of your being where God waits for you, ready to listen to you, to guide and support you. Let this be a time of rest and relaxation with God, free from concerns, responsibilities, and emotions.

At the end of the guided meditation, the sound of the ringing of the bowl will draw you back gently to this place and time. (Ring the bowl)

Feel your body resting wherever you are, in a chair with feet flat on the floor and your hands open in your lap, or on the ground sitting comfortably on a pillow, or lying down. Notice where there is tension in your body and allow it to release as you are held in this sacred space.

Begin three full breaths on your own and then return to normal breathing and rest. (Count in, one, two, three, four, hold; release, one, two, three, four, hold; repeat). (Ring the Tibetan Harmony Bowl) Slowly increase your breathing as you move your fingers and toes. Gently bring your awareness back to the circle and when you are ready, open your eyes.

Guided Meditation #2

"God in My Breath"

adapted from Sadhana *by Anthony de Mello*

Close your eyes and imagine that the air you are breathing in is charged with the power and presence of God. Think of the air as an immense ocean surrounding you – an ocean that is filled with God's strength, supporting and carrying you. Be aware that you are drawing in the power and presence of God each time you breathe in. Notice how your body responds as it is filled again and again. As you release all concerns and cares into the vast ocean around you, feel your body becoming lighter, expanding and merging with Divine presence. Imagine your whole body becoming radiantly alive through breathing in God's life-giving Spirit. Bring this awareness back with you as you slowly begin to open your eyes.

Gathering

1. Welcome and ask everyone to wear name tags again if necessary.

2. Ask if anyone would like to place something on the altar, inviting their explanation.

3. Light the candle. Take a few minutes for silence and centering, using Guided Meditation #3. Review the meditative experience by reading the following:
<u>Be</u> – Focus energy and attention on the breath, the conscious awareness of the tactile closeness of God in the present moment.
<u>Hear</u> – Bring full awareness to sounds and listen for the silence between the sounds. Notice the stillness out of which all emerges.
<u>Now</u> – Notice how you are physically present, releasing tension and stress. When we are consciously breathing, hearing and attending to the now, we are fully present to our divine nature, allowing God to move through us.

4. Ask everyone to answer two questions briefly:
Were you able to approach your days with sacred segmenting? (See Journey 1)
Were you able to find a time each day for quiet prayer or meditation?

Presenting the Theme

1. Take turns reading the "Introduction to Meditation and Contemplative Prayer," and allow for questions. (see pp. 8–9)

Prayer

1. Experience Lectio Divina using the adapted form of Psalm 139. (see pp. 10–11)

2. While playing meditative music, ask individuals to journal about what they experienced or learned. Recommended music: "Per crucem" canon by Taize.
They may refer to the processing questions in Journey 1.

3. Share thoughts and feelings as a group. Members should always feel comfortable choosing not to comment.

4. Play Guided Meditation #4, "The Celtic Hand Meditation." This is an embodied form of prayer with a focus on movement within the body.

Closing

1. End with a blessing – "I am secure in the flow of graceful good," from <u>Blessings</u> by Julia Cameron, p. 1.

New References
Brandt, Leslie. <u>Psalms Now</u>. St. Louis: Concordia Publishing House, 1973.
Cameron, Julia. <u>Blessings</u>. New York: Penguin Putnam Inc., 1998.
Farrell, Edward. <u>Celtic Meditations</u>. Denville, New Jersey: Dimension Books, 1976.
Kaisch, Ken. <u>Finding God</u>. New Jersey: Paulist Press, 1994.
<u>Taize Alleluia</u> CD Chicago: GIA Publications, 1988.

Introduction to Meditation and Contemplative Prayer

Isaiah 30:15
In returning and rest you shall be saved; in quietness and trust shall be your strength.

Psalm 46:10
Be still and know that I am God.

"Meditation and contemplation are vehicles for effectively moving us out of our self-centered frame of reference; we learn to see through His eyes. Our lives will be transformed by these experiences so that the suffering in which we clothed ourselves falls away. Through meditation and contemplative prayer, we move out of doing and into being, away from the secular into the sacred. And by means of this movement, we become the holy people we were created to be.

By meditation, we mean those techniques which make some use of discursive thought to go beyond the thought itself. For example, we can use thought to create an image of Jesus and to dwell on that image. Contemplation, on the other hand, does not use discursive thought. Contemplative prayer is a radical abandonment of discursive thinking in the effort to experience what lies beyond. Because contemplative prayer is so different from what we ordinarily do, it is important first to learn the steps of meditation which lead up to the contemplation of God." *Kaisch, Ken. Finding God, pp. 22 & 26*

Four Forms of Prayer

Four forms of prayer are incorporated into the Journeys. As suggested by Kaisch in Finding God, meditation is experienced first, followed by a progression of prayers that will build the capacity to enter into the stillness of contemplative prayer.
The four forms are Lectio Divina, Focusing Prayer, the Jesus Prayer, and Centering Prayer:

1. Lectio Divina

Lectio Divina is a method of prayer that goes back to the fourth and fifth centuries. Translated as "sacred reading," it is a way of praying with scripture through meditation. It was a monastic practice brought to the West from the Eastern desert fathers by John Cassian at the beginning of the fifth century. It has been closely connected to Benedictine spirituality since its development and popularity began in the communities of monks founded by St. Benedict. The process includes listening to the same scripture being read three times, each time opening to new personal awareness and insight. (experienced in Journeys 2 and 14)

2. Focusing Prayer

Focusing prayer attends to our bodies in order to access inner truth about our experiences and reality. It is a reverent listening to open to ourselves in a caring way. It was developed by Eugene Gendlin in 1982. He believed that in being faithful to our bodies, we are being faithful to the body of Christ and His incarnation. As we touch the benevolent wisdom of our interior, we can feel grace moving in our body. If we are willing to listen, we will be given the gift of wisdom and insight. Often we can experience an inner release and a sense of moving towards resolution in our bodies.
(experienced in Journeys 2, 6, and 13)

3. The Jesus Prayer

"Lord Jesus Christ, have mercy on my soul."

The Jesus Prayer is a monologistic prayer that repeats the same phrase over and over in one's mind throughout the day. It is a good bridge between meditation and contemplation because it begins in thought, but eventually leads to an automatic response without effort. It becomes part of the pattern of one's life to focus on petitioning God for mercy and guidance. This "praying without ceasing" is rooted in ancient Christian tradition and leads to a sense of grace pouring into one's heart. The Jesus Prayer was revived in 1861 by an unknown Russian pilgrim who wrote about his experience of using "Lord Jesus Christ, have mercy on my soul" in The Way of the Pilgrim. Other religious traditions use this method of creating a personal mantra to bring the Divine deeply into consciousness.
(experienced in Journey 8)

4. Centering Prayer

Centering prayer was developed by Father Thomas Keating in the mid-1970's at the Cisterian abbey of St. Joseph in Spencer, Massachusetts. Responding to the spiritual poverty of our times, he wanted to make the riches of contemplative life available to the lay person who could not spend life in a monastery. It is a contemporary revision of the technique that was first presented in the fourteenth century in The Cloud of Unknowing (author unknown) which described an emptying of all thought, images, and emotions in prayer. Father Keating added the choosing of one sacred word to assist in focusing on sitting in God's Holy Presence.
(experienced in Journey 12)

Psalm 139

O God, You know me inside and out,
    through and through.
Everything I do,
    every thought that flits through my mind,
    every step I take,
    every plan I make,
    every word I speak,
You know, even before these things happen.
You know my past:
    You know my future.
Your encompassing presence covers my every move.
Your knowledge of me sometimes comforts me,
    sometimes frightens me;
but always it is far beyond my comprehension.

There is no way to escape You, no place to hide.
If I ascend to the heights of joy,
    You are there to meet me.
I could fly to the other side of our world
    and find You there to lead the way.
I could walk into the darkest of nights,
    only to find You there
To lighten its dismal hours.

You were present at my very conception.
You guided the molding of my unformed members
    within the body of my mother.
Nothing about me, from beginning to end,
    was hid to Your eyes.
How frightfully, fantastically wonderful it all is!

May Your all-knowing, everywhere-present Spirit
    continue to search out my feelings and thoughts.
Deliver me from that which may hurt or destroy me,
    and guide me along the paths of love and truth.

adapted from <u>Psalms Now</u>, *by Leslie Brandt, pp. 211 & 212*

Praying Psalm 139 through Lectio Divina

One person in the group reads out loud:

1. The Psalm is read three times with a pause of 2-3 minutes between.
   a. Read slowly asking to notice which word or phrase draws one's attention.
   b. Read a second time noticing what feelings or images arise about this phrase.
   c. Read a third time asking how these words, images and feeling might apply to one's life today.

2. Process individually with journaling or drawing and then share as a group.

Guided Meditation #3

Be – Hear – Now

Let the sound of the Tibetan Harmony Bowl draw you deep within to a place of peace and rest. (Ring the bowl) Focus your attention and your energy on your breath. Breathe deeply to the count of four, with the in-breath equal to the out-breath. Let this conscious awareness of your breath fill you with the tactile closeness of God in the present moment.

Bring your awareness to any sounds around or within you. Listen to the silence between the sounds. Notice and feel the stillness out of which all emerges.

Be aware of your physical presence; wherever your body is touching the chair or the floor and allow it to relax into that place. Release the places of tension or stress that you notice in your body by breathing into them.

As you are consciously breathing, hearing, and attending to your body, be fully present to the now of your divine nature. Allow the grace of God's presence to move through you.

Let the ringing of the bowl bring you gently back to the circle. (Ring the bowl)

Guided Meditation #4

Celtic Hand Meditation

adapted from <u>Celtic Meditations</u>, *by Edward J. Farrell*

Rest comfortably with your eyes closed and hands open, resting in your lap, with palms up. Tune into your breathing, relax tension points and move into your center. Become aware of the air at your fingertips, between your fingers and on the palm of your hands. Experience the fullness, strength and maturity of your hands. Think of your hands, think of the most unforgettable hands you have known – the hands of your father, your mother, and your grandparents. Remember the oldest hands that have rested in your hands. Think of the hands of a newborn child; your nephew, your niece or your own child – the incredible beauty, perfection, and delicacy in the hands of a child. Once upon a time your hands were the same size.

Think of all that your hands have done since then. Almost all that you have learned has been through your hands – turning yourself over, crawling and creeping, walking and balancing yourself, learning to hold something for the first time; feeding yourself, washing and bathing, dressing yourself. At one time, your greatest accomplishment was tying your shoes.

Think of all the learning your hands have done and how many activities they have mastered, the things they have made. Remember the day you could write your name. Our hands are not just for ourselves but for others. How often they were given to help another. Remember all the kinds of work they have done, the tiredness and aching they have known, the cold and the heat, the soreness, the bruises. Remember the tears they have wiped away, our own or another's, the blood they have bled, the healing they have experienced. How much hurt, anger, and violence they have expressed, and how much gentleness, tenderness, and love they have given. How often they have folded in prayer; a sign both of their powerlessness and of their power. Our father and mother guided these hands in the great symbolic language of our hands – the sign of the cross, the striking of our breast, the handshake, the wave of the hand in hello or goodbye.

There is a mystery which we discover in the hand of a woman or the hand of a man that we love. There are the hands of a doctor, a nurse, an artist, a conductor, a priest; hands which you can never forget.

Now raise your right hand slowly, and gently place it over your heart. Press more firmly until your hand picks up the beat of your heart, that most mysterious of all human sounds, one's own heartbeat, a rhythm learned in the womb from the heartbeat of one's own mother. Press more firmly for a moment and then release your hand and hold it just a fraction of an inch away from your clothing. Experience the warmth between your hand and your heart. Now lower your hand to your lap very carefully as if it were carrying your heart. For it does. When you extend your hand to another, it's not just bone and skin, it's your heart. A handshake is the real heart transplant.

Think of all the hands that have left their imprint on you. Fingerprints and handprints are heartprints that can never be erased. The hand has its own memory. Think of all the people who bear your heartprint. They are indelible and will last forever.

Now, without opening your eyes, extend both your hands on either side of you and find another hand. Don't simply hold it, but explore it and sense the history and mystery of the hand. Let your hand speak to it and let it listen to the other. Try to express your gratitude for this hand stretched out to you in the dark and then bring your hand back again to your lap. Experience the presence of that hand lingering on your hand. The afterglow will fade but the print is there forever.

Whose hand was that? It could have been any hand; it could have been His hand. It was. He has no other hands than ours.

Gathering

1. Welcome and arrange the altar.

2. Light the candle for a few minutes of silence and centering – lead a quieting exercise with slow, rhythmic breathing. The breath is to be followed with the mind, imaging God's loving energy flowing to every part of the body, releasing tension and stress. Breathing in calm, breathing out love. You may play Guided Meditation #1.

3. Ask the two questions that will be used in the remaining journeys:
   How are you in body/mind/spirit today?
   What has been your experience of God since we last met?

Presenting the Theme

1. Take turns reading the selections on "Soul Friends/Soul Circles" and "The Experience of Soul Friends." Allow a moment of silence between each reading so that it can be absorbed and considered. (see pp. 14–15)

Prayer

1. Ask individuals to go deep within to recall a soul friendship. Encourage them to experience again an interaction with this person as deeply as possible, remembering feelings, the surroundings and the impact on them. Play Guided Meditation #5.

2. Ask them to write and then draw about the experience. Play meditative music for 5 – 10 min. Recommended music: "Can You Feel the Love Tonight?" on the Lion King CD.

3. Offer opportunity for group members to share their experience and insight.

4. Introduce Tai Chi and teach some basic movements. (see pp. 16–17) Play Guided Meditation #14 for verbal instructions.

5. Use these movements to honor soul friendships with Tai Chi.
Recommended music: Josh Groban CD, "The Prayer."

Closing

1. Read "A Friendship Blessing" from Anam Cara. (see p. 17)

New References
Josh Groban CD. Reprise Records, 2001.
Kelly, Thomas. A Testament of Devotion. San Francisco: Harper Brothers, 1941.
Lion King CD. Walt Disney Records, 1994.
Miller, Jean & Stiver, Irene. The Healing Connection. Boston: Beacon Press, 1997.
O'Donohue, John. Anam Cara. New York: HarperCollins, 1997.
Sellner, Edward. The Wisdom of the Celtic Saints. Notre Dame: Ave Maria Press, 1993.

Soul Friends/Soul Circles

"In the early Celtic church, a person who acted as a teacher, companion, or spiritual guide was called an anam cara or "soul friend." It originally referred to someone to whom you confessed, revealing the hidden intimacies of your life. With the anam cara you could share your innermost self, your mind and your heart. This friendship was an act of recognition and belonging. When you had an anam cara, your friendship cut across all convention, morality, and category. You were joined in an ancient and eternal way with the "friend of your soul." The Celtic understanding did not set limitations of space or time on the soul. There is no cage for the soul. The soul is a divine light that flows into you and into your other. This art of belonging awakened and fostered a deep and special companionship." *O'Donahue, John. Anam Cara, pp. 13 & 14*

"In a chaotic world, friendship is the most elegant, the most lasting way to be useful. We are, each of us, a living testament to our friends' compassion and tolerance, humor and wisdom, patience and grit. Friendship, not technology is the only thing capable of showing us the enormity of the world." *Deitz, Steven. The Lonely Planet*

"The stories and sayings of the Celtic saints clearly reveal that mentoring and spiritual guidance were considered an important if not essential part of Celtic Christian spirituality. All the saints seem to have been changed profoundly by these relationships – whether their mentors were human or angelic, and whether they offered a compassionate ear or a challenging word. They were keenly aware, as are many today, that inner healing happens when we openly and honestly acknowledge to another person our concerns, grief, and spiritual diseases, and that God is very close to those who speak as friends do, heart to heart." *Sellner, Edward. Wisdom of the Celtic Saints, p. 27*

"People feel enhanced and fulfilled when they can be actively engaged together about something that feels vital. Participating together in this way is very different from struggling alone without a sense of impact or response, or, alternatively, feeling that you have to hold back parts of yourself because you don't know where the other person is psychologically. This is what we mean by building increasing mutual empathy and mutual empowerment. Together we now had more resources – more energy, action, knowledge, sense of worth, and sense of connection – in relationship. At these moments of interchange, a person moves into more connection based on her more real representation of her experience." *Miller & Stiver. The Healing Connection, p. 133*

"Two people, three people, ten people may be in living touch with one another through Him who underlies their separate lives. This is an astounding experience, which I can only describe but cannot explain in the language of science. But in vivid experience of divine Fellowship, it is there. We know that these souls are with us, lifting their lives and ours continuously to God and opening themselves, with us, in steady and humble obedience to Him. It is as if the boundaries of our self were enlarged, as if we were within them and as if they were within us. Their strength, given to them by God, becomes our strength, and our joy, given to us by God, becomes their joy." *Kelly, Thomas. A Testament of Devotion, "The Blessed Community"*

The Experience of Soul Friends

Centered in God	Guide from birth to death	Confessor
Affection	Sees our gifts/possibilities	Mutuality
Common vision	Affirmation	Challenge
Soul Making	Not limited by time & space	Sanctuary & rest
Speaking from heart	Healing	Facing suffering
Life giving energy	No separation even though distant	

Guidelines for Being a Soul Friend

1. Listen with mind and heart: show empathy, encourage, share, and confront
   Don't: fix, protect, rescue, control, or carry another's feelings

2. Feel: congruent, relaxed, free, aware of reality, high self worth
   Not: tired, anxious, fearful, liable, blamed, vulnerable, and inadequate

3. Concerned with: relating person-to-person, not to the situation
   Not: the solution, answers, circumstances, being right, details, performance

Expect that each person has the ability to use the best in them to make decisions and take responsibility for their own actions, that each of us has enough to make it on our own with the movement of God in our lives.

Qualities of a Healing Presence

Physical presence	Body to body	Seeing, touching, doing, hearing
Psychological presence	Mind to mind	Assessing, communicating, writing, reflecting, non-judging, accepting, empathizing, confidentiality, trusting, mindfulness in the moment, positive thinking, forgiving
Spiritual presence	Spirit to spirit Whole being to whole being Centered self to centered self	Centering, meditating, imagery, at-one-ment, openness, communion, loving, appreciating, knowing, connecting, intentionality, recognizing inner Divine beauty, intuition, mystery, faith

An Introduction to Tai Chi

Tai Chi is an ancient Chinese system of exercise and a way of life, integrating the mind, body, and spirit. It embodies the Taoist principles of Yin and Yang, ebb and flow. Although it can be used as a martial art, it also is a powerful meditative practice. Use the following exercises as a way to embody your own experience and prayer. A suggestion is that the movement on the "in" breath be a prayer offering and the movement on the "out" breath be a thanksgiving or blessing.

Begin with feet, shoulder width apart and knees slightly bent. Your arms are bent with hands facing down and gently resting at the hips. This is Mountain Pose. Use slow and continuous movements with the body relaxed. Once you have learned the movements, they can be joined in a graceful exercise. Breathe in with the motions of lifting. Breathe out with the motions of lowering. Use your imagination to give meaning to the movements and you will find it as a wonderful tool to immerse you in the blessings of the present moment.

Basic Movements – #14 on the CD

Cloud Hands

Float your arms out to your sides as if they are rising gently on a cloud of air. Continue to bring your arms overhead so that your palms are facing crown of head. As you lift your arms, breathe in slowly and fully. Exhale slowly and completely as you press your palms toward the floor in front of your body. As you lift, your knees straighten slightly. As you lower, your knees bend slightly. Imagine that your hands are floating on a cloud. Let your body move effortlessly as you image the peace of God moving through you.

Lotus Blossom

With arms down, bring your hands together so that your index fingers are touching in front of your body with wrists relaxed. Plant a seed in the earth. Image what you would like to grow within you. Slowly draw a line up the center of your body continuing over your head. Follow the movement of your hands with your eyes, watching the seed grow into a plant. As you reach the top, open your hands toward heaven. As the blossom opens at the crown of your head, offer it as a prayer or gift to God. Allow your arms to float out to the sides and down, returning to the starting position. Breathe in slowly and deeply as you lift, breathe out slowly and completely as you lower.

Holding Up Heaven

Stand with your legs shoulder width apart and knees soft. Bend forward to the ground with cupped hands, fingers facing inward. Gather in a large circular motion and raise your arms until your palms face crown of head. Follow your hand movement with a soft gaze. Turn your palms toward the heavens and raise arms overhead to support heaven as a pillar. Float your arms down toward the side. Image gathering strength from the earth, asking in prayer for what you need. As you reach toward heaven, offer your gifts to God.

Grinding Corn

Begin in Mountain Pose. Move your weight to the right foot as you draw a clockwise circle with your right hand, inhaling. Your hands are waist high with palms facing down. Move your weight to the left as you draw a counter-clockwise circle with your left hand, breathing out. Both feet stay on the ground. It is a gentle shifting of weight as you create a repetitive motion. Begin by drawing small circles. The circles can become larger and larger as you shift more weight from side to side. As you move freely, image tending and caring for those you love and for all of creation.

A Friendship Blessing

May you be blessed with good friends.

May you learn to be a good friend to yourself.

May you be able to journey to that place in your soul where there is great love, warmth, feeling and forgiveness.

May this change you.

May it transfigure that which is negative, distant, or cold in you.

May you be brought into the real passion, kinship, and affinity of belonging.

May you treasure your friends.

May you be good to them and may you be there for them; may they bring you all the blessings, challenges, truth, and light that you need for your journey.

May you never be isolated.

May you always be in the gentle nest of belonging with your anam cara.

from Anam Cara, by John O'Donahue

Guided Meditation #5

Recalling a Soul Friend

Follow the sound of the Tibetan Harmony Bowl to draw your consciousness inward to the place of peace and rest within where God waits for you. (Ring the bowl) Breathe deeply and feel your body releasing all tension and totally resting. There is nothing to do, nothing to worry about. You only need to rest and be restored.

As you rest in this place of perfect peace, recall a time with a person who was a soul friend to you. Image that person's physical presence, their face, their body, what they are wearing. Remember how it felt to be in their presence.

Where are you with this person? Remember the details of the setting. What is around you, what are the colors, sounds or smells in this scene?

What are you doing? Are you talking to each other or are you sharing a time of silence? Recall the sound of your friend's voice. Ask them if they have a message for you.

Deepen your recollection of this time together and savor it. Reflect on why this was so meaningful to you. What did you learn about yourself? How did it help you? How can it bring meaning to your life now?

Offer a prayer of gratitude for this person and realize that such a deep connection of two souls never ends. At the sound of the ringing of the bowl, bring the joy of this connection back with you to the present moment. (Ring the bowl)

Gathering

1. Welcome and arrange the altar.

2. Light the candle for a few minutes of silence and centering, leading the quieting exercise with slow rhythmic breathing. Consider repeating Guided Meditation # 3.

3. Ask the two questions:
   How are you in body/mind/spirit today?
   What has been your experience of God since we last met?

Presenting the Theme

1. Take turns reading the selections on "The Divinity of Everyday Life." Allow a pause between each one for individual reflection. (see pp. 20–22)

Prayer

1. Play "The Deer's Cry" from The Pilgrim CD for individuals to meditate to music on the Celtic Christian concept of being continually surrounded by the love and protection of God. The words to the music appear on p. 23.

2. Introduce the Poetry, Prayer, and Blessings forms, asking individuals to write a blessing for their own life using one of the examples or their own form. Allow about 10 – 15 minutes. Play meditative music – suggested is Enya Watermark CD. (see pp. 24–25)

3. Give individuals the opportunity to share their writing.

4. Introduce and teach the "Five Elements" of Tai Chi meditation as a way to incorporate the awareness of all the blessings of their daily lives into their consciousness through movement. Practice the movements without music and then with "The Deer's Cry." (see pp. 26–28). An illustration of the movements is included and oral directions are #15 on the CD.

Closing

1. As a blessing, use one or two of the participants' writings, or read "I am alert to my blessings" from Blessings, by Julia Cameron, p. 50.

New References
Bender, Sue. Plain and Simple. San Francisco: HarperCollins, 1989.
De Waal, Ester. The Celtic Way of Prayer. New York: Bantam Doubleday, 1997.
Enya Watermark CD. New York: Reprise Records, a Time Warner Co., 1988.
Huang, Chungliang. Embrace Tiger Return to Mountain. Berkeley: Celestial Arts, 1987.
Kisly, Lorranine. Ordinary Graces. New York: Bell Tower, 2000.
O'Donahue, John. Eternal Echoes. New York: HarperCollins, 1999.
The Pilgrim CD. Dublin: Tara Music Co. Ltd., 1994.
Newell, Philip J. Listening For the Heartbeat of God. New York: Paulist Press, 1997.
Carmichale, Alexander. Carmina Gadelica III. Scottish Academic Press, 1976.

The Divinity of Everyday Life

To see a World in a grain of sand
And a Heaven in a wild flower,
Hold Infinity in the palm of your hand
And Eternity in an hour.
"Auguries of Innocence" by William Blake

...I know nothing else but miracles,
Whether I walk the streets of Manhattan,
Or dart my sight over the roofs of houses toward the sky,
Or wade with naked feet along the beach just in the edge of the water,
Or stand under trees in the woods,
Or talk by day with anyone I love, or sleep in bed at night with anyone I love,
Or sit at table at dinner with the rest,
Or look at strangers opposite me riding in the car,
Or watch honeybees busy around the hive of a summer forenoon,
Or animals feeding in the field,
Or bird, or the wonderfulness of insects in the air,
Or the exquisite delicate thin curve of the new moon in spring,
These with the rest, one and all, are to me miracles,
The whole referring, yet each distinct and in its place.
To me every hour of the light and dark, is a miracle,
Every cubic inch of space is a miracle,
Every square yard of the surface of the earth is spread with miracles,
Every foot of the interior swarms with miracles.
Walt Whitman

"From this center (the place that ironically I guess they knew better than many of us do today in spite of all the help available to us in the techniques and technologies of self-knowledge!) there comes this vivid sense of a God who knows, loves, supports, is close at hand, and actually present in their lives. Of course this sense of divine presence and protection are found elsewhere in the history of the Church, but I feel that nowhere else is it found with quite the same intensity. It is one of the many gifts of the Celtic tradition to us, and perhaps the most important. Of course they also know God as transcendent, and they write quite superbly of God as the creator God, all-powerful, all knowing. But they also know that he is present here and now in the world that he has made." *De Waal, Ester. The Celtic Way of Prayer, p. 70–71*

God's Word is in all Creation,
visible and invisible.
The Word is living, being, spirit,
all verdant greening,
all creativity...
Hildegard of Bingen

"As the days passed, I felt I was living in a still-life painting. In the background was a soft, sweeping farm landscape, and in the foreground were many people, all busy doing their chores with silent grace. Everything was ritual. Doing the dishes, mowing the lawn, baking bread, quilting, canning, hanging out the laundry, picking fresh produce, weeding. No distinction was made between the sacred and the everyday." *Bender, Sue. Plain and Simple, p. 50*

"Faith does not simply account for the unknown, tag it with a theological tag and file it away in a safe place where we do not have to worry about it. On the contrary, faith incorporates the unknown into our everyday life in a living, dynamic and actual manner. The unknown remains unknown. It is still a mystery, for it cannot cease to be one. The function of faith is not to reduce mystery to rational clarity, but to integrate the unknown and the known together in a living whole, in which we are more and more able to transcend the limitations of our external self." *Kisly, Lorranine. Ordinary Graces, p. 119*

"In these the lights of the skies, the sun and moon and stars, are referred to as graces, the spiritual coming through the physical, and God is seen as the Life within all life and not just as the Creator who set life in motion from afar. It was particularly during my time at the Abbey on Iona, where many of these prayers had been forged and developed, that I became further convinced that this tradition of prayer is an important resource for the whole Church, for it makes the connection that is so often lacking between spirituality and the whole of life. Here, then, within the treasury of Christianity itself, was a rich stream of prayer that gave expression to something like the creation awareness that is being awakened among all sorts of people throughout the world today. And so I came to see that the prayers in the old Celtic tradition could aid our search for a spirituality that seeks God by looking toward the heart of life, not away from life.

So to look to God is not to look away from life but to look more deeply into it. Together with this emphasis on the presence of God at the heart of creation, of God being the heartbeat of life, there is also a sense of the closeness, the personal immediacy of God to us, a closeness not only of God but of the whole host of heaven, enfolding the earth and its people with love." *Newell, Philip. Listening For The Heartbeat of God, pp. 4 & 48*

The goodness of sea be thine,
The goodness of earth be thine,
The goodness of heaven be thine.
The grace of the love of the skies be thine,
The grace of the love of the stars be thine,
The grace of the love of the moon be thine,
The grace of the love of the sun be thine.

A Blessing from the Carmina Gadelica III, p. 233

Matins

I.

Somewhere, out at the edges, the night
Is turning and the waves of darkness
Begin to brighten the shore of dawn.

The heavy dark falls back to earth
And the freed air goes wild with light,
The heart fills with fresh, bright breath
And thoughts stir to give birth to colour.

II.

I arise today

In the name of Silence
Womb of the Word,
In the name of Stillness
Home of Belonging,
In the name of the Solitude
Of the Soul and the Earth.

I arise today

Blessed by all things,
Wings of breath,
Delight of eyes,
Wonder of whisper,
Intimacy of touch,
Eternity of soul,
Urgency of thought,
Miracle of health,
Embrace of God.

May I live this day

Compassionate of heart,
Gentle in word,
Gracious in awareness,
Courageous in thought,
Generous in love.

John O'Donahue, Eternal Echoes

The Deer's Cry

I ARISE TODAY
through the strength of heaven
light of sun
radiance of moon
splendor of fire
speed of lightening
swiftness of wind
depth of the sea
stability of earth
firmness of rock

I ARISE TODAY
through God's strength to pilot me
God's eye to look before me
God's wisdom to guide me
God's shield to protect me
From all who shall wish me ill
afar and near
alone and in a multitude
against every cruel merciless power
that may oppose my body and soul

Christ with me
Christ before me
Christ in me
Christ beneath me
Christ above me
Christ on my right
Christ on my left
Christ when I lie down
Christ when I arise
Christ to shield me
Christ in the heart of everyone
Who thinks of me
Christ in the mouth of everyone
Who speaks to me

I ARISE TODAY

Anon 8th Century

Poetry, Prayer and Blessings

Blessing the Ordinary

Blessing the ordinary can be playful.

Write a blessing for an ordinary task, or something in your life that may be taken for granted or seems mundane (i.e. all that goes into computer work; or the telephone, or a chore).

Example:
Bless to me my little car, O God.
Bless to me my driving.
Bless the anticipation of my car taking me to my destination.
Bless the feel of my getting into the seat.
Bless the seat for its support of my body while I drive.
Bless the steering wheel upon which I place my hands.
Bless the…(etc.)

Repetitive Phrasing

Write a prayer or blessing using the repetitive phrase throughout.

There are several ways to get started.

a) First, find a phrase you'd like to repeat. Then, write the prayer, letting the phrase shape the prayer. (make up your own phrase, or look to Scripture or Psalms).

b) Write a prayer first. Then, look for a phrase within the prayer to repeat every so often throughout. (It may tend to expand and enlarge the prayer).

c) Take some time to sit quietly. Allow the silence to still any thoughts. In silence, see if a phrase comes to you. Let the prayer flow out of this experience.

d) Choose a place in nature. Allow your gaze to settle on some aspect of creation. Use that subject to focus your repetitive prayer.

Examples of repetitive phrasing:

I arise this morn to….	*Bless to me my hands, that they may…*
I arise this morn to…	*Bless to me my feet, that they may…*
In the strength of Christ, I…	*In the midst of dark powers…*
In the love of Christ, I…	*In the midst of fearful thoughts…*
In the wisdom of Christ, I…	
The beauty of creation upholds…	*…heal the wounds within you.*
The majesty of creation strengthens…	*…heal the wounds within you.*
The mystery of creation invites…	*…release new life within you.*
	…release new life within you.

Cinquain – One Subject
Line 1 Subject: one word
Line 2 Two words that expand and enlarge the subject
Line 3 Three words, or a three-word phrase that describes the subject
Line 4 A short sentence about the subject
Line 5 A one-word synonym or example of the subject

Example:

Creation
God's Handiwork
Earth, water, sky
We are born here, live, and die
Home

This and That – Two Subjects
First select Subjects A and B. Suggestions: opposites i.e. heaven and earth; persons and nature
Line 1 Subject A: one word
Line 2 Two words that expand and enlarge the subject
Line 3 Three words describing subject A
Line 4 Four words that describe both subjects
Line 5 Three words describing Subject B
Line 6 Two words that expand and enlarge the subject
Line 7 Subject B: one word

Examples:

Jesus	*Tree*
Brother, healer	*Hearty, strong*
Lover, challenger, reconciler OR	*Necessary, living, beautiful*
Embodied, faithful, teacher, friend	*Fluid, supple*
Creative, giver, enthusiast	*Water*
Sister, seeker	
Janet	

LIMERICKS – usually humorous
Rhyming scheme: AABBA – all As rhyme with each other; Bs rhyme with each other

_ _ _ _ _ _ _ **A** ,   Do you know of a church known as Trinity?
_ _ _ _ _ _ _ **A** ,   It will be on Lake Drive to infinity.
_ _ _ _ _ **B** ,   It is a church without walls
_ _ _ _ **B** ,   Ed and Jerry take calls
_ _ _ _ _ _ _ **A** ,   In an effort to improve our divinity.

Moving with the Five Elements of Tai Chi

"Tai Ji exemplifies the most subtle principle of Taoism, known as wu-wei. Literally, this may be translated as "not doing," but its proper meaning is to act without forcing – to move in accordance with the flow of nature's course which is signified by the Tao, and is best understood from watching the dynamics of water." *(Huang, p. 2)*

"When energy stores inside of us without natural release, we build up tension. Since energy is a continuous source of being alive every day, we must learn to be with it, to release it when necessary and to regenerate it." *(Huang, p. 18)*

"Everything that is happening in your body comes from one source. That same settling feeling that we call tai, the middle-centered feeling in your physical/mental self. If you are constantly in touch with that source as you move, then the outside forces around your moving body, all that is happening around you, will become a part of your sphere of movement." *(Huang, p. 5)*

Use the imagery of **Fire**, **Water**, **Wood**, **Metal**, and **Earth** to create a moving meditation to bless all aspects of life. (see illustrations) Play #15 on the CD.

1. Begin with your feet parallel and your knees slightly bent. Use your arms to scoop energy from the earth into a circle in front of your body, gathering up all of your life. Bring your hands to your heart, honoring your life.

2. Use your hands to open your heart by parting them and reaching out to your sides as in parting a curtain. Ask in prayer for balance and harmony in your life as you look from one hand to the other. Your arms are gently moving up and down.

3. Reach up with the left hand for sky energy and down with the right hand for earth energy. Mix these energies in a circular movement in front of your center and bring them into the belly.

4. In one continuous movement, step back onto the left foot and then forward onto the right foot as the arms go up and forward, sending out energy like fire. Offer all you are as a gift to God. Exhale strongly.

5. Shift back onto the left foot while slowing bringing your hands down in a gentle waving motion all along the sides of your body. Image the Divine cooling your body with water as a blessing. Rest and be in a receptive mode by bending your knees.

6. Begin a slight turn to the left and then turn to the right one and one-half circles. Use your arms to gather wood or new forms of life and growth. While turning, image being a tree with reaching branches. Ask for and receive what you need from God.

7. Return to the front position, turning slightly to the right as metal is gathered by scooping your right hand down in back of you and then up into your center. Scoop again to the left and mix the metal in front of your body in a circular motion using both hands. Image creating something new and then bring your hands together and bend down to release your creation into the earth.

8. Begin again by raising your hands up to the sky, asking for new life. Bring your hands down in a curve and pull up energy from the earth. Release this up and out, skyward.

9. Cross your hands at the wrist, palms towards your face, embracing the tiger or all aspects of life. Give thanks for your life as it is.

10. Bring the hands down slowly to the side, returning to mountain pose.

11. Repeat all the movements again but begin on the other side; reach for sky with the right hand and earth with the left hand; step back with the right foot and forward with the left; begin to turn to the right and then go one and one-half turns to the left; scoop left and then right.

Moving With the Five Elements of Tai Chi

1a. Circle   1b. Focus   2. Open and Balance   3a. Connect Earth and Sky

3b. Mixing   4. Fire – Send Up   5a. Water – Bring Down   5b. Start to turn back

6. Gathering – 1 ½ times (front)   (back)   (front)
(back)

7a. Gathering   7b. Metal Mixing   7c. Earth Letting Go

8a. Beginner's Mind   8b. Pull Up   8c. Out Skylight

9. Embrace Tiger   10. Return to Mountain

28

Gathering

1. Welcome and arrange the altar.

2. Light the candle for a few minutes of silence and centering, leading the quieting exercise with slow rhythmic breathing. Breathing in light, breathing out peace.

3. Ask the two questions:
How are you in body/mind/spirit today?
What has been your experience of God since we last met?

Presenting the Theme

1. Take turns reading the selections on "Spiritual Journeys." Allow a pause between each one for individual reflection. (see pp. 30-31)

Prayer

1. Play Guided Meditation #6.

2. Allow time to first journal and then draw about the experience of the guided meditation. The writing and drawing activate both the right and left brain.

3. Process the experience as a group with each member sharing what they have drawn or written. (see p. 3 for processing questions)

4. Explain the process of Life Mapping, referring to the attached worksheet. This will be done on their own time at home, to be shared with the group at The Retreat. The written part of exploring their spiritual experience is done first. Then they decide which are the most important elements to include on a map. Next, a visual map is created using a metaphor for their life. For example a gardener may use a garden, or a canoeist could use a river. They do not have to be an artist to do this. Some people use abstract symbols, stick figures, or stickers to represent their themes and events. Answer any questions and make sure everyone is clear on the process. This is not meant to be a timeline, but is a creative way to experience and share one's life. (see p. 32) (see p. 36 for a visual example of a life map)

Closing

1. Read "My Life is But a Weaving." (see p. 33)

New References
Downey, Michael. Understanding Christian Spirituality. New Jersey: Paulist Press, 1997.
Hess, Herman. Siddhartha. New York: Bantam Books, 1951.
Oldfield, David. The Adolescent Spiritual Journey. Washington, D.C.: The Foundation For Contemporary Mental Health, 1987.
Palmer, Parker. Let Your Life Speak. San Francisco: Jossey-Bass Inc., 2000.
Pearson, Carol S. Awakening The Heroes Within. San Francisco: HarperCollins, 1991.
Rice, Howard L. A Book of Reformed Prayers. Louisville: Westminister John Knox Press, 1998.

Spiritual Journeys

"Self-understanding; self-love lays at the groundwork for spiritual experience."
James Carse, Director of Religious Studies at New York University

Hebrews 11:8,10

By faith Abraham obeyed when he was called to set out for a place that he was to receive as an inheritance; and he set out, not knowing where he was going. For he looked forward to the city that has foundations, whose architect and builder is God.

"A helpful guide in charting out the contours of a specifically Christian Spirituality within the context of the more common and universal striving for personal integration is Karl Rahner (1904 –1984), one of the most significant Christian theologians of this century. Briefly, Rahner envisioned the gift and task of personal integration in terms of self-transcendence: giving oneself and finding oneself in the experience of knowledge, freedom, and love. Rahner recognized human experience as a locus of God's revealing self-disclosure." *Downey, Michael. Understanding Christian Spirituality, pp. 32–33*

"All spiritual journeys involve an experience of metanoia, a 'change of heart.' The ordeals faced on the road of trials do not occur because God is somehow mean-spirited, but because it takes such difficult events for us humans to see through the many illusions on which we base our lives. We are called upon to die to that strictly-secular way of looking at our lives, so we might live in the larger truth of spirit." *Oldfield, David. The Adolescent Spiritual Journey, p. 1*

"Peregrinatio (a Celtic spiritual journey) is not undertaken at the suggestion of some monastic abbot or superior but because of an inner prompting in those who set out, a passionate conviction that they must undertake what was essentially an inner journey. Ready to go wherever the Spirit might take them, seeing themselves as hospites mundi, "guests of the world," what they are seeking is the place of their resurrection, the resurrected self the true self in Christ, which is for all of us our true home. So peregrinatio presents us with the ideal of the interior, inward journey that is undertaken for the love of God." *De Waal,Ester. The Celtic Way of Prayer, p. 2*

"Finding the great story that informs your life is a sacred task. To know your story is to know who you are. It is not to be taken lightly, although it does not have to be unduly heavy either. If you know your own great story, you are much less likely to sell yourself short, to get confused by the inessential, or to let others manipulate you or talk you into being less than you could be. Identifying your own great story (or stories) helps you to find something of your own specialness in a way that helps you understand the significance of your own life. No one but you can tell this story because you are the only one who knows what you are here to do or to learn." *Pearson, Carol. Awakening The Heroes Within, p. 28*

"From that hour Siddhartha ceased to fight against his destiny. There shone in his face the serenity of knowledge, of one who is no longer confronted with conflict of desires, who has found salvation, who is in harmony with the stream of events, with the stream of life, full of sympathy and compassion, surrendering himself to the stream, belonging to the unity of all things." *Hess, Herman. Siddhartha, p. 14*

"But for others, and I am one, the poet's words will be precise, piercing, and disquieting. They remind me of moments when it is clear – if I have eyes to see – that the life I am living is not the same as the life that wants to live me. In those moments I sometimes catch a glimpse of my true life, a life hidden like the river beneath the ice. And in the spirit of the poet, I wonder: What am I meant to do? Who am I meant to be? Then I ran across the old Quaker saying, "Let your life speak." I found those words encouraging, and I thought I understood what they meant: "Before you tell your life what you intend to do with it, listen for what it intends to do with you. Before you tell your life what truths and values you have decided to live up to, let your life tell you what truths you embody, what values you represent." *Palmer, Parker. Let Your Life Speak, pp. 2–3*

Prayer for All of Life

God of our life, through all the circling years,
We trust in thee;
In all the past, through all our hopes and fears,
Thy hand we see.
With each new day, when morning lifts the veil,
We own Thy mercies, Lord, which never fail.

God of the past, our times are in Thy hand;
With us abide.
Lead us by faith to hope's true promised land;
Be Thou our guide.
With Thee to bless, the darkness shines as light,
And faith's fair vision changes into sight.

God of the coming years, through paths unknown
We follow thee;
When we are strong, Lord, leave us not alone;
Our refuge be.
Be thou for us in life our daily bread.
Our heart's true home when all our years have sped.

by Hugh Thomson Kerr

Rice, Howard. A Book of Reformed Prayers, p. 105.
From the Presbyterian Church (U.S.A.)
The Presbyterian Hymnal, 1990

31

Creating a Life Map
Mapping the Past

Oldfield, David. The Journey. The Foundation For Contemporary Mental Health, 1987

People (friends, relatives, acquaintances who have influenced you; characters from books and films; heroes and role models, enemies you've had; "guides" you've used; loves; people you are indebted to and those who "owe" you, etc.):

Events and Experiences (your most powerful memories: the happiest day of your life; your most embarrassing moment; accidents; good times/bad times with family and friends; the hardest decision you've ever made, the biggest mistake you've made; the crises you've survived; the nicest thing anyone has ever done for you, etc.):

Emotional "Landscapes" (memories of love, hate, anger, terror, wonder, compassion; fears you've faced and run from; insecurities and satisfactions, etc.):

Words To Live By (advice – good and bad – you remember, song lyrics that have guided your actions, etc.):

Hopes and Dreams (what you wanted to be when you grew up; favorite fantasies; wishes you've made; future fantasies, etc.):

Frustrations and Disappointments (unmet expectations: things that "didn't work out" etc.):

My Life is But a Weaving

My life is but a weaving.
Between my Lord and me.
I do not choose the colors,
God knows what they will be.
For God can view the pattern
From the upperside,
And I can see it only
From the underside.
Sometimes God weavest sorrow,
It seemest strange to me
But I will trust God's presence
And work on faithfully.
'Tis God who fills the shuttle
and God knows what is best,
So I will work in earnest
And leave to God the rest.
Not 'til the loom is silent
And the shuttle ceases to fly,
That God will unroll the canvas
And we'll know the reason why…
The dark threads are as needful
In the skilled weaver's hand,
As the gold and the silver,
In the pattern God has planned.

Author unknown

Guided Meditation #6

A Spiritual Journey

Allow the sound of the Tibetan Harmony Bowl to draw your awareness inward as you close your eyes, directing them down toward your heart. (Ring the bowl) Feel your body relaxing as you imagine being held in a Divine embrace. Follow your deep rhythmic breathing with your mind, bringing in the light of God to fill all the cells of your body. Exhale peace, radiating it outward in ever-growing circles.

As you settle into a place of deep rest, the image of a doorway or gate appears. Notice what kind of opening it is. What is it made of and how do you open it? You are being called to open the door as an invitation to begin a new journey with God. Open the door and step across the threshold, becoming aware of what is presented to you.

What are you seeing? Watch as the details become very clear. Awaken all your senses so that you enter more fully into this world. Listen carefully. What are you hearing? Are you called to touch something? What is it and how does it feel? Is there anything to taste or smell? Allow yourself the time to fully experience what is offered to you. When you are complete with taking in all that you have found, a pathway will appear. What does it look like? Begin to walk down the path, noticing what it is made of and all that you see along the way. You may meet animals and people who speak to you. Remember what they say. You will go around a bend and suddenly find an obstacle blocking your way. What is it? At first you may feel unable to continue, but you, either alone or with the help of others, discover a way through or around the obstacle. What do you do to overcome it?

As you continue to follow the path, you become even more aware of your strength and power. You will see more clearly and feel more deeply. You come to the end of the path and find an inviting place to stop. Sit down to rest and someone very important to you will appear. What does this person say or do? Enjoy this time together and then thank your companion for joining you on the path.

Take the time to recall all that you have experienced and learned to bring back with you to the present moment. At the ringing of the bowl, bring your attention slowly back to the circle. (Ring the bowl)

Preparation

1. Send information about the retreat in advance with directions for how to get to the location. Include a fee to cover the cost of the facility and food if necessary. It is best to have everyone bring food. Remind group members to bring their Footprints of the Soul book and their life maps.

Gathering

1. Upon gathering at the retreat setting, familiarize everyone with the facility and organize the food for lunch and snacks. Take a short walk outside to bring a sense of the natural world into the gathering.

2. Create an altar by placing a table at the center of a circle of chairs and arrange anything that group members have brought on the table.

3. Gather in a circle for a time of centering and silence. Light the altar candle. Use "The Prayer Within" as the opening meditation. (see p. 38)

4. Ask the two questions:
   How are you in body/mind/spirit today?
   What has been your experience of God since we last met?

Sharing of Life Maps

1. Ask for volunteers to present their life maps. Half of the group will present in the morning and half after lunch. A presentation should take about 15 minutes. Ask group members to use "holy listening," honoring and holding in prayer each person's life map. Other than asking brief questions for clarification or saying thank you, no comments are made.

Individual Reflection and Prayer

1. Introduce a time for individual prayer and reflection. For one hour, each person should walk or find a place outside to rest and experience the presence of the Divine in the natural world. During this time ask that they bring back something from nature that drew their attention. These will be used to create a closing meditation. Agree on a time to return and share lunch. Extinguish the altar candle as members leave the circle.

Lunch

1. Share lunch for about one-half hour.

Sharing of Life Maps

1. Return to the circle for the presenting of the remaining life maps. Relight the altar candle. Ask for a moment of centering and silence before beginning. The remaining participants share their life maps.

2. Thank everyone for sharing their life stories. Read Teilhard de Chardin's "Trust in the Slow Work of God" as closure to the sharing of life maps. (see p. 39)

Example

Individual Reflection

1. Ask them to journal personally about what they brought back from their prayer time outside. What message does it have for you? How does it represent you? How does it honor your life experience? Extinguish the altar candle.

Break

1. Take a break for about 20 minutes for snacks and moving around.

Final Gathering and Closing Prayer

1. Ask the group to bring their object from the natural world to the altar for the closing ceremony.

2. Relight the altar candle and ask for a time of centering and silence. As participants place their offerings from nature on the center table, ask them to share the meaning they hold.

3. Read "The Person Next to Me." Each participant should read a section as it is passed around the circle. (see p. 40)

4. Read Ecclesiastes as the closing blessing.

Ecclesiastes 3:1-8

For everything there is a season, and a time for every matter under heaven:
A time to be born, and a time to die;
A time to plant, and a time to pluck up what is planted;
A time to kill, and a time to heal;
A time to break down, and a time to build up;
A time to weep, and a time to laugh;
A time to mourn, and a time to dance;
A time to cast away stones, and a time to gather stones together;
A time to embrace, and a time to refrain from embracing;
A time to seek and a time to lose;
A time to keep, and a time to cast away;
A time to rend, and a time to sew;
A time to keep silence, and a time to speak;
A time to love, and a time to hate;
A time for war, and a time for peace.

5. Listen to "Deep Peace" from the Celtic Twilight CD as a closing blessing.

New References
Douglas, Bill. "Deep Peace." Celtic Twilight CD. San Francisco: Hearts of Space, 1994.
Rupp, Joyce. Birthings and Blessings.

The Prayer Within: A Breath Prayer

To discover your breath prayer, follow these five easy steps:

Step One

Sit in as comfortable a position as possible. Then be calm and quiet. Close your eyes and remind yourself that God loves you and that you are in God's loving presence. Recall a favorite passage from scripture that places you in the proper frame of mind. "Be still, and know that I am God" (Psalm 46:10) is a line people often find helpful.

Step Two

As you keep your eyes closed, imagine that God is calling you by name. Listen carefully and hear God asking you: "(Your name), what do you want?"

Step Three

Answer God with whatever comes honestly from your heart. Your answer may be a single word, such as peace or love or forgiveness. Your answer may instead be a phrase or brief sentence, such as "I want to feel your forgiveness" or "I want to understand your love" or "I want to be with you." Whatever your response is, it becomes the heart of your prayer.

Step Four

Chose your favorite name for God. Choices people commonly make include God, Jesus, Christ, Lord, Spirit, Shepherd, or Creator.

Step Five

Combine your name for God with your answer to God's question, "What do you want?" and you have your prayer. For example:

What I want	Name I call God	Possible prayer
peace	Lord	Let me know your peace.
love	Jesus	Let me feel your love.
rest	Shepherd	Let me rest in thee.

adapted from The Breath of Life, *by Ron Delbene pp. 12–13*

Above all, trust in the slow work of God,
We are, quite naturally,
impatient in everything to reach the end
without delay.
We should like to skip
the intermediate stages.
We are impatient of being
on the way to something unknown,
something new.
And yet it is the law of all progress
that it is made by passing through
some stages of instability,
and that it may take a very long time.

And so I think it is with you.
Your ideas mature gradually –
let them grow,
let them shape themselves,
without undue haste.
Don't try to force them on,
as though you could be today
what time (that is to say, grace and
circumstances acting
on your own good will)
will make you tomorrow.

Only God could say what this new spirit
gradually forming within you will be.
Give our Lord the benefit of believing
that his hand is leading you,
and accept the anxiety of
feeling yourself in suspense and incomplete.

Teilhard de Chardin

The Person Next to Me

Look around you, look around. Who is the person sitting next to you?

The person next to me is the greatest miracle, the greatest mystery I will ever meet at this moment, a live example of the WORD-MADE-FLESH of God's continuing presence in the world, of God's continuing "coming" into our midst.

The person next to me is an inexhaustible resource of possibilities – and only some of those resources have been tapped.

The person next to me
is a unique universe of experience
is a combination of needs and possibilities, dread and desire, smiles and frowns, laughter and tears, fears and hopes, all struggling to find expression.

The person next to me is bursting to become something special, to arrive at some destination, to have her story known.

The person next to me has problems and fears, wonders "How am I doing?", is often undecided and disorganized, and painfully close to chaos.

But is endowed with a great toughness in the face of trouble, able to survive the most unbelievable difficulties.

But the person next to you can never be fully understood. She is more than any description or explanation.

For the person next to you is a mystery... As the WORD MADE FLESH is a mystery and dwelt among us. So look around you; for God is here.

Look around you sisters and brothers, look around. Who is the person sitting next to you?

For the person next to you is mystery – just as you – too – are mystery. So much of what we see is only the shell surrounding depths within that even we fail
to know, to understand, to appreciate.

So much of what we identify as "Me" is only the casing holding within – a mystery that only God knows and loves fully.

And only when we have the courage to break open the hard shell of ourselves will we ever truly know and love who we are.

This breaking open is sometimes easy, sometimes painful, sometimes sudden, sometimes a crack at a time. And frequently we are unable to open up without someone else's help.

Joyce Rupp

Gathering

1. Welcome and arrange the altar.

2. Light the candle for the time of centering and silence.

3. Ask the two questions:
   How are you in body/mind/spirit today?
   What has been your experience of God since we last met?

Presenting the Theme

1. Take turns reading the selections on "Letting Go." Allow a moment of silence between each reading so that it can be absorbed and considered. (see pp. 42–43)

2. Introduce the information on Focusing Prayer and discuss. (see p. 44) Refer to Journey 2, p. 9 for a definition.

Prayer

1. Play Guided Meditation #7 which is a directed focusing prayer.

2. Ask individuals to journal about their experience, writing about the information their bodies may have offered to them. When they are finished, ask them to consider the things they can't control and the things that they can change. They can make two columns to sort through and write down their concerns:

   <u>things I can't change</u>   <u>things I can change</u>

3. Teach the simple Yoga Prayer of Release. (see p. 45)

4. Lead them in moving through the release prayer several times to music. They can turn over each of the concerns to God, and ask for help and strength to change what they can. Recommended music – "Magnificat" canon by Taize (CD used in Journey 2)

Closing

1. Close by standing in a circle, holding hands and saying the "Serenity Prayer." (see p. 43)

New References
St. Romain, Philip. <u>Reflecting on the Serenity Prayer</u>. Missouri: Liguori, 1997.
May, Gerald G. <u>Will and Spirit</u>. San Francisco: HarperCollins, 1982.
Gendlin, Eugene. <u>Focusing</u>. New York: Everest House, 1978.
Tucker, Lucy Abbott-Tucker. "Live Nearby, Visit Often. Focusing and the Spiritual Direction Process."
   <u>Presence: The Journal of Spiritual Directors International</u>. Vol. 7: 3.
Mira, Mira & Shyam Mehta. <u>Yoga The Iyengar Way</u>. New York: Alfred A. Knopf, 1995.

Letting Go

"What, then, is this spiritual peace, shalom, or serenity? Put simply, it is a deep, inner sense that all is well. The experience goes beyond our systems of emotional or rational intelligence. Rather it is intuitive or spiritual knowing that produces in us the inner experience of calmness, clarity, and awareness. In serenity, we can live more fully in the now moment, perceiving in acceptance the reality presenting itself without wanting to control things to gratify our selfish desires. There is no need to have or get anything more than what the moment presents; living in serenity itself is sufficient.

All is well in God's world. When we realize this through our faith connection with God, we experience serenity. We can lose serenity, however, by neglecting to nurture our faith. During such times we are thrown back upon our own resources. Anxious preoccupation returns along with the willful desire to manipulate the world and other people to conform to our own deluded model of happiness. We need to see how we do this, and we have to give up on worldly peace. We need only return to God, entrusting our lives to God's care, and peace will return in short order. If we do this daily, serenity will grow." *St. Romain, Philip. Reflecting On the Serenity Prayer, pp. 2 & 5*

Philippians 4:6-7

Do not worry about anything, but in everything by prayer and supplication with thanksgiving let your request be made known to God. And the peace of God, which surpasses all understanding, will guard your hearts and your minds in Christ Jesus.

"Willingness and willfulness cannot be explained in a few words, for they are very subtle qualities, often overlapping and very easily confused with each other. But we can begin by saying that willingness implies a surrendering of one's self-separateness, an entering into an immersion in the deepest processes of life itself. It is a realization that one already is part of some ultimate cosmic process and it is a commitment to participation in that process. In contrast, willfulness is the setting of oneself apart from the fundamental essence of life in an attempt to master, direct, control, or otherwise manipulate existence. More simply, willingness is saying yes to the mystery of being alive in each moment. Willfulness is saying no, or perhaps more commonly, Yes, but..."
May, Gerald. Will and Spirit, p. 6

"Be patient to all that is unsolved in your heart and try to love the questions themselves, like locked rooms and like books that are now written in a very foreign tongue. Do not now seek the answers, which can not now be given you because you would not be able to live with them. And the point is, to live everything. Live the questions now. Perhaps you will then gradually, without noticing it, live along some distant day into the answer." *Maria Ranier Rilke*

Letting Go

To a dear one about whom I have been concerned.

I behold the Christ in you.

I place you lovingly in the care of the Father.

I release you from my anxiety and concern.

I let go of my possessive hold on you.

I am willing to free you to live your life
according to your best light and understanding.

Husband, wife, child, friend –

I no longer try to force my ideas on you, my ways on you.

I lift my thoughts above you, above the personal level.

I see you as God sees you, a spiritual being, created
in His image, and endowed with qualities and abilities
that make you needed, and important – not only to me
but to God and His larger plan.

I do not bind you, I no longer believe that you do not have
the understanding you need in order to meet life.

I bless you,
I have faith in you,
I behold Jesus in you.

Author unknown

"The Serenity Prayer"

"God, give us grace to accept with serenity
the things that cannot be changed,
courage to change the things which should be changed,
and the wisdom to distinguish the one from the other."

Reinhold Niebuhr 1943

Focusing Prayer

"When we live close to the interior feeling responses we have to the circumstances in our life, visit them often with a sense of welcome and care, we are then able to move more graciously in life. While we may often be somewhat aware of the feelings associated with life events, the difference in focusing is in the way we listen and attend to the feelings. Rather than trying to strong-arm them into something different, forget them until access to their energy is lost, or offer them to God, in focusing we care for the feelings and listen carefully to their divine wisdom. When we can extend a hospitable welcome to the deeper feelings within our own experiences, allowing them to speak, sing and dance, they carry the potential to help to transform from the 'inside out.' The person takes an inventory of those things that are taking up space in the interior. I often describe this as looking around inside and noticing what concerns and experiences are preoccupying their time and attention. Sometimes there are many; often there are just three or four. When one takes inventory during the focusing process, he or she is not 'taking care' of those experiences, but simply acknowledging their presence. Naming them and setting them aside for a few moments enables people to see what else is happening inside and creates a feeling of spaciousness within. What happens is a sorting process, as the person looks through all that has been named and chooses the one that needs some attention and care.

Focusing is a body-centered experience. We want to notice and carefully attend to how the body is carrying the experiences of life, wherein we find real wisdom. When a person attends to the feelings of life in this way, it is truly a sacred moment. If a person is reverent to whatever is real inside by simply allowing it to be, an incredible gift of love is being given to the feelings. The inner experience responds with receptivity and generosity." *Tucker, Lucy-Abbott. "Live Nearby, Visit Often."* Presence, The Journal of Spiritual Directors International. *Vol.7: no.3, pp. 7–9*

The Focusing Steps

1. Preparing – growing quiet, going within, becoming aware of your body's language.

2. Finding space by taking an inventory. Ask yourself: What is taking up space inside of me right now?

3. Feeling/sensing/choosing which one is number one. Allowing the issue or feeling to make itself known.

4. Asking your body, "Is it okay to be with this?" If yes, go to the next step. If no, have a caring presence for not wanting to be with it. Choose another area and try again.

5. Letting go into it with caring presence. Just being with it, sensing the whole of it.

6. Allowing it to express itself, revealing more in words, images, memories, or feelings.

7. Nurturing of self, savoring what has come, and saying thank you.

Yoga

Yoga is a means of developing inner awareness, introspection, and intimacy with the self. It means the union of opposites, and brings the body, mind, and spirit into harmony. Yoga increases our awareness of our innate wholeness, giving a sense of well- being and peace. It is a psychophysical technology that was developed centuries ago by Hindu spiritual aspirants who needed to strengthen and energize the body for long hours of meditation. It is recorded in the Vedas, a Hindu religious text, from the second century A.D. Because practicing Yoga centers our consciousness within and develops inner strength and tranquility, it can be a form of prayer. Our body is stretched and strengthened as tension is released, freeing hidden wellsprings of energy.

Yoga Prayer of Release

1. Begin standing with your weight evenly distributed between your feet, knees slightly bent. Image a line of light above your head coming from heaven, running through your body and going down into the earth between your feet. Feel firmly connected to above and below.

2. Place your hands in a prayer position, palms together, over your heart. This is the Namaste position. "Namaste" is a Sanskrit word that means: "I honor the place in you where God resides, which is of love, of truth, of light, and of peace. When you are in that place in you and I am in that place in me, we are one."

3. Bring to mind what concerns you want to release, and raise your arms up above your head. Spread your hands wide apart and feel the concern lifted from your heart. Breathe deeply.

4. Bring your hands together above the head, palms forward, and slowly bring them to the ground in a forward bend. Lead with your heart or the center of the chest and look forward. Keep your knees bent as much as is needed. Gather strength from the earth and give thanks. Bow your head.

5. Come up slowly, bringing your arms up and out at your sides, like wings. Return to the Namaste position.

6. Repeat several times, letting go of one concern or several. Move at your own pace. After learning the movement, close your eyes if you wish.

Guided Meditation #7

Letting Go: A Focusing Prayer

Focus your awareness on your body, noticing the sensations being expressed. Allow all tension to release by breathing deeply and rhythmically into the stressed areas of your being. As you grow quiet and feel the stillness, go deep within to listen to the language of your body.

Trust your intuition to choose an area in your body to attend to and allow it to surface. What is the issue connected to this sensation in your body? Ask permission to work with it. If the answer is no, surround it with a caring presence and let it go. Then choose another area of your body on which to focus.

If the answer is yes, fill the area with unconditional love and just be with it as the issue reveals more to you. How is it expressing? What are the colors, images, words, memories or feelings that are surfacing? Receive and attend reverently to what comes, sensing the inner release.

Take the time to nurture yourself, savoring what has come to you. Express gratitude for the new sense of spaciousness within. As you return slowly to the circle, bring back with you the information you have received by attending to the language of your body.

Gathering

1. Arrange for the group to meet at a labyrinth. I suggest finding an outdoor experience if possible. If this is not available, there are indoor, portable labyrinths that can be used. Allow about two hours for the experience that includes an introduction, the walking, and processing after the experience.

2. Welcome and create sacred space in the center of the labyrinth by forming a circle, holding hands, and offering a prayer. Give thanks for the opportunity to journey with God, and ask that each person experience the presence of God.

Presenting the Theme

1. Gather outside the labyrinth to read "Walking the Labyrinth." (see pp. 48–49)

2. Prepare the group to walk the labyrinth by doing the following:
   Quiet the mind; consider what your life circumstances are now; ask a question, or ask for guidance; focus your mind by repeating a short mantra, or favorite piece of scripture.

3. As you enter the labyrinth:
   Experience feelings and inner thoughts without judgment; let your body move spontaneously; pay attention to your breath; If walking outside, notice what the natural world is showing you; make this a personal experience. If you pass another person, greet with a smile and refrain from speaking.

Prayer

1. Ask group members to enter the labyrinth separately with space between each one. Each person will have different timing. Explain that when they are finished, they will journal and draw about their experiences in their <u>Footprints of the Soul</u> book. Designate the area near the labyrinth where they can do this.

2. If walking an indoor labyrinth, play meditative music during the labyrinth portion, as well as during the journaling and drawing time. Suggested CD: <u>Transformation at Assisi</u>.

3. Process the experience by asking participants to share what they have written and drawn.

Closing

1. Close by reading the poem, "The Labyrinth," by Carolyn Joy Adams as a blessing. (see p. 50)

New References
Artress, Lauren. <u>Walking A Sacred Path</u>. New York: Berkley Publishing, 1995.
Shulman, Richard. <u>Transformation at Assisi</u> CD. Rich Heart Music, 1992.
West, Melissa Gayle. <u>Exploring the Labyrinth: A Guide for Healing and Spiritual Growth</u>.
   New York: Broadway Books, 2000.

Walking the Labyrinth

"Walking the labyrinth fulfills six important contemporary needs: deepening spirituality; inwardness and connection; access to intuition and creativity; simplicity; integration of body and spirit; and intimacy and community."

West, Melissa, *Exploring the Labyrinth*

Passages from <u>Walking A Sacred Path</u> by Lauren Artress

"To walk a sacred path is to discover our inner sacred space; that core of feeling that is waiting to have life breathed back into it through symbols, archetypal forms like the labyrinth, rituals, stories, and myths." (p. 15)

"Why does the labyrinth attract people? Because it is a tool to guide healing, deepen self-knowledge, and empower creativity. Walking the labyrinth clears the mind and gives insight into the spiritual journey. It urges action. It calms people in the throes of life transitions. It helps them see their lives in the context of a path, a pilgrimage. They realize that they are not human beings on a spiritual path but spiritual beings on a human path." (p. 21)

"When we are grounded in our bodies, we are stabilized and can receive information more accurately. Much like fine-tuning a radio, if we are attuned to our bodies the static in the incoming messages and impulses is reduced. To reclaim the body is a sacred act. In doing so, we may discover a path to the Divine. Dancing, skipping, crawling, or solemnly walking are all encouraged on the labyrinth. The more free and spontaneous we are in the labyrinth, the more energy we bring into our lives." (p. 141)

"Sacred space is by definition the place where two worlds flow into each other, the visible with the invisible. The finite world touches the infinite. In sacred space we can let down our guard and remember who we are. The rational mind may be released. In sacred space we walk from chronos time to kairos time, as we allow our intuitive self to emerge." (p. 155)

The Labyrinth at the Episcopal Cathedral of Christ The King Kalamazoo, Michigan

The labyrinth symbolizes the journey to the center or to the self, the life journey or the path of life, or the spiritual journey – our walk with God. It is also said to represent the ongoing cycle of life, death, rebirth and the process of transformation and healing.

You may think of walking the labyrinth in three stages:

<u>Purgation</u> – a releasing, a letting go of the details of your life. This is an act of shedding thoughts and emotions. It quiets and empties the mind as you walk into the labyrinth.

<u>Illumination</u> – may occur when you reach the center. Stay there as long as you like. It is a place of meditation and prayer. Receive what is there for you to receive.

<u>Union</u> – which is joining God, the divine healing force at work in the world. Each time you walk out of the labyrinth you become more empowered to find and do the work for which your soul is longing.

The Labyrinth

Your life is a sacred journey.
And it is about change,
    Growth,
        Discovery,
            Movement,
                Transformation.
Continuously expanding your vision of what is possible.
    Stretching your soul.
        Learning to see clearly and deeply.
            Listening to your intuition.
            Taking courageous risks.
Embracing challenges at every step along the way…

You are on the path…
    Exactly where you are meant to be right now…

And from here,
    You can only go forward,
Shaping your life story into a magnificent tale of triumph,
    Of healing,
        Courage,
            Beauty,
                Wisdom,
                Power,
                      Dignity and love.

Carolyn Joy Adams

Gathering

1. Welcome and arrange the altar.

2. Light the candle for the time of centering and silence.

3. Ask the two questions:
   How are you in body/mind/spirit today?
   What has been your experience of God since we last met?

Presenting the Theme

1. Explain the steps of the watercolor meditation and distribute the art materials.

Prayer

1. Read each step of the process, allowing time for each person to finish.

2. Play meditative music while each person contemplates their own visual representation. Suggested music: "Circle of Life" on the Lion King CD

3. Ask participants to write a short mantra or repetitive phrase like "The Jesus Prayer." (see Journey 2) They can use words that came to them as they contemplated their watercolor, or portions of scripture, or other prayer. Examples might be:
   Gracious God, heal my heart;
   Lord, make me an instrument of thy peace;
   I am rooted and grounded in love;
   or Divine Creator, fill me with your light.
Ask that they repeat this phrase as often as possible for the next two weeks. They can speak it out loud, or repeat it silently in their minds as they go about their day. Ask them to journal about how reciting the prayer is impacting them during this time.

Closing

1. Close by standing in a circle as group members offer the prayers or mantras they have written as a blessing to the group.

Meditative Watercolor Workshop

Created by Christine C. Woomer

This workshop uses watercolor and a guided meditation process to explore feelings that promote the honoring of each individual's sacredness and power in the universe.

Supplies: Watercolors, Brushes, Water, Paper Towels (for blotting brushes)
        9 2" square white papers per person (plus extras)
        8 1/2" X 11" colored paper per person
        Tape, paste or glue

To begin, create a sacred place by welcoming everyone, lighting a candle and having a moment of silence.

The guide begins softly:

"I will be guiding you through a watercolor meditation. Absolutely no experience with paints is necessary. We will use several different techniques, which I promise are simple and I will walk you through each step. An example is included at the end of the journey.

These steps may seem deceptively simple. The physical act of putting paint on paper is simple so that you may enjoy the process, yet remain focused on each of your intentions.

You will paint nine little squares. There is no such thing as a mistake. However, if you wish to change what you started for any reason, please feel free to take another square and begin again. Let's begin.

Take a paper square, feel it, smell it, turn it over, notice its thickness. For such a small piece of paper, it has great significance. This small square of paper signifies your own truth, your inner heart of hearts, the divine within each of you. In fact, white is the color that denotes truth and purity.

In this moment, you hold in your power the chance to understand your truth more fully.

With watercolors, the paper, which signifies truth, always shines through. Without truth, nothing can follow. You must respect your truth first and foremost, just as with watercolors the paper is essential.

1. Now let's use the first square of paper, water, and paints to signify the energy that radiates out into the universe from your center.

To do this, first coat the paper with water. Then choose a color and paint the center of your square. You can paint a shape or just a dot in the center. Notice how the color radiates out. Add more water or color if you wish. This represents your energy reaching out into the world, effecting the world.

2. Our second exercise represents the energy you are receiving. Again, coat the second square of paper with water. Pick one or more colors and paint only the border of the square. Notice the colors bleeding toward the center. Imagine your heart, or center receiving this colorful energy and wisdom. Add more water and colors as you feel the need.

3. Think about two things that you would like to blend more efficiently or for the first time, two things in your life that have maybe been at odds that you would like to connect somehow. Choose a color for each. Again, wet the third square of paper. Paint a stripe on one side of the square with one color and paint the other side with the second color. With your brush help the colors move toward each other. See how they bleed and move toward each other to create a third color, a communion. You have just made this blending happen.

Visual images are a great way to understand your feelings. Sometimes feelings and thoughts are so elusive and hard to make sense of. If you create a 'visual' of some kind for yourself, often you are able to analyze and understand more clearly. You can actually get your mind around a scary or complex situation. Create your own vocabulary with colors and shapes. In watercolors, you place these on your truth (paper) and the results are kernels or flashes of wisdom.

4. Your fourth square will symbolize a softening of an anger or hurt that you have experienced. First pick a color and apply it in a symbol of your own making to the dry paper. This color and the actual applying of it, represents its power over you. Now saturate your brush with water and wash over it. See how the edges soften and blur. See how its color and intensity fades. This represents your own power over these hurts or angers that live in you. You can choose to give them less importance by 'flooding' or brushing them out.

5. The fifth square will represent the enrichment that your heart craves. Think about a goal that you want to reach. Assign it a color. Paint this color as lightly as you can using a lot of water over your entire square. As it dries, think about the journey necessary to achieve your goal. Your next step is to increase the intensity of your 'goal color' in small steps. Add a bit more color to your square and paint over all of it but a small strip at the top. You want to preserve each step to your goal to remind you of everything it took to 'arrive.' Paint as many 'bands' as you need to, to reach your 'pure color' goal on the opposite end of your square.

This demonstrates that your goals are attainable. You must be patient and take all the necessary steps, but understand it is absolutely within your reach. You can actually see that now. This makes it 'real.'

6. Using the sixth, seventh and eighth squares, take some time to paint them to represent some aspect of your life today. You might choose: Chaos, Calm, Happiness, Love, Friends, Places, God, Water, Fire, Earth, Wind, Nature, Prayer or anything else that may come to mind.

7. Using the ninth square, you are ready to paint your 'Center,' all that makes up you today. Start with a base coat of a light color, and add, and add, and add, symbols and colors until you realize the 'richness' of who you are. Add as many components as you wish. 'BE FREE.' Just represent yourself today: your truth, your loves, your goals, what life has given you, your energy, your wisdom, you're blending of power and truth to create a whole.

Now as you gaze upon your works of art, see how complicated you are, how much you have learned and how you consist of so many colors and layers! Arrange your squares around your last 'CENTER' painting. Attach them to your choice of colored paper with tape rolls or paste.

This 8 1/2" x 11" work of art is a saturated picture of you. It holds your dreams, hopes and your power. Put this in a frame to behold. You can display it anywhere, as no one can decipher your personal code or meaning except you. It is a personal diary that is 'out in the open' now. It has been given the power of visual integrity. You can use any medium to help you explain yourself to others, work things out or celebrate wonderful happy feelings. Look around at the stunning array of diaries. Creating a visual document of how you feel or what you think automatically bestows importance on that piece of you, in essence, honoring all that you are.

Blessings to all.

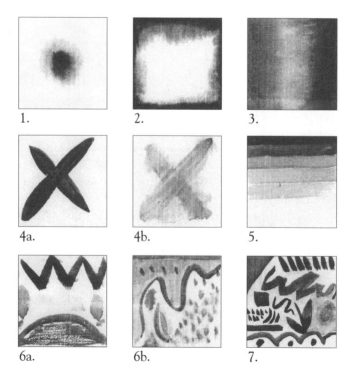

1.

2.

3.

4a.

4b.

5.

6a.

6b.

7.

Gathering

1. Welcome and arrange the altar.

2. Light the candle for a few minutes of silence and centering.

3. Ask the two questions:
   How are you in body/mind/spirit today?
   What has been your experience of God since we last met?

Presenting the Theme

1. Take turns reading the selections from "Opening the Heart." Allow a pause between each one for individual reflection. (see pp. 56–57)

Prayer

1. Ask them to silently reflect on their own heart as "Will You Come Home?" on the <u>When October Comes</u> CD is played.

2. Play Guided Meditation #8.

3. Share the new information about the heart from <u>The Heart's Code</u>. (see p. 58)

4. Introduce Healing Touch by taking turns reading the selections about it. (see pp. 58–59)

5. In pairs, partners share what they would like for the healing of their hearts.

6. The partners take turns using their hands to heal and bless each other with Healing Touch. (see attached directions p. 60)

7. Play "New Dawn" on the <u>Mystic Harp</u> CD during the Healing Touch.

Closing

1. Close in a circle by reading "I open my heart to love with an open hand" from <u>Blessings</u> by Julia Cameron, p. 9.

New References

Graham, Litt & Irwin. <u>Healing From the Heart</u>. Canada: Wood Lake Books, 1998.

Pearsall, Paul. <u>The Heart's Code</u>. New York: Broadway Books, 1998.

Smith, Linda. <u>Called Into Healing</u>. Colorado: HTSM Press, 2000.

Thomas, Zach. <u>Healing Touch: The Church's Forgotten Languauage</u>.
   Louisville: Westminister John Knox Press, 1994.

Burke, Susie. "Will You Come Home?" <u>When October Comes</u> CD. Rounder, 1991.

Opening the Heart

Song of Songs 8:6-7
Set me as a seal upon your heart, as a seal upon your arm; for love is strong as death, passion fierce as the grave. Its flashes are flashes of fire, a raging flame. Many waters cannot quench love, neither can floods drown it. If one offered for love all the wealth of his house, to buy love, it would be utterly scorned.

"I think continually of those who were truly great..... The names of those who in their lives fought for life, who wore at their hearts the fire's center." *Stephen Spencer*

"I feel within me a consuming fire of heavenly love which has burned up in my soul everything that was contrary to itself and transformed me inwardly into its own nature." *William Law*

> "May we learn to open in love so all the doors
> and windows of our bodies swing wide on
> their rusty hinges.
> May we learn to give ourselves with both hands,
> to lift each other on our shoulders
> to carry one another along.
> May holiness move in us so we pay attention to its
> small voice and honor its light in each other."

Dawna Markova

"If I'm quiet and still enough, I can feel you living through me. I recognize your spirit stirring memories, emotions and desires. Sometimes I look out on my world as if my eyes are windows to our common soul. I share this with you in gratitude and love. Always." *Christian de Quincey to his parents*

"Bless your heart. A heart that is blessed blossoms, opening up to more joys, pleasures, compassion and love, creating a warmly glowing spirit from which love flows through and around, from person to person freely like air." *Edie Jurmain*

A Hopeful Prayer

"Stream of Love
all encompassing
Gathering me
as a cherished one
in welcoming embrace

Stream of Compassion
bonding with me
holding my tears
in a tender cup
of your love

Stream of Goodness
pouring your light
into my soul
like a sunbeam
at dawn

Stream of Nurturance
providing for me
in the darkness
of your protective
enveloping womb

Stream of Joyfulness
dancing in me
celebrating life
with each moment
of gladness

Stream of Hope
ever glorious
ever present
kissing my vision
and enriching my dreams"

Joyce Rupp

The Heart's Code

Paul Pearsall, an author and psychoneuroimmunologist, was director of a psychological clinic for the rehabilitation of cardiac transplant patients. He researched the relationship of the brain, immune system, and life events. The following information is adapted from his book, The Heart's Code:

1. Princeton University has researched the energy of the heart for over 20 years in the PEAR Project.

2. The research suggests a fifth force of energy emanating from the heart that can transcend and travel with the other known forms of energy.

3. The heart is the most powerful muscle in the body, beating 100,000 times a day. Energetically, the brain revolves around the heart.

4. Like the brain, the heart has its own nervous system and releases neurochemicals that convey information to cellular receptors throughout the body. It also has receptors that store information.

5. Heart cells pulsate, exchanging information with other systems within the body and also with other living systems.

6. The heart's electromagnetic field is 5 thousand times more powerful than that created by the brain; 250 cycles/second compared to 30 CPS.

7. The hands are natural conductors of energy with hundreds of sweat glands that act as electrodes.

Healing Touch Spiritual Ministry: an energy based approach to healing
using the laying on of hands. It is effective with hands touching the body or with hands two to three inches off the body.

"Healing Touch, in my experience, is ministry at its highest level. It is about responding to that inner voice that calls one to be God's instrument, to act out of a compassionate heart with no attachment to the outcome. It is about being a vessel, a conduit, an instrument, a channel, and a courier through which God can act in another's life. It's about being in the "flow" of God's grace.

Healing Touch Spiritual Ministry brings the work to those who wish to use it within a spiritual setting such as church ministry. It can enhance the work of parish nursing, church healing ministries, pastoral care in hospitals and nursing homes, spiritual direction, retreats, hospice care, and home health care, to name a few. It can be used within families wishing to bring wholeness back into their relationships."

Smith, Linda. Called Into Healing, p. 10

"We did not realize the extent to which hearts are linked with hands in communicating compassion. A 'hands off' Christianity splits us from our bodies and feelings. When compassion does not flow through us, refreshing us in the very act of obedience, we block spiritual energy. Long ago Christians expected physical cures to accompany the laying on of hands in baptism, communion, and special services for the sick. What does happen more commonly is a 'tremendous transformation of faith' that enables people to live more fully regardless of the outcome of their physical illness.

As a result of healing touch, the first Christians expected not simply bodily healing but a deeper wholeness: strength, forgiveness of sins, vivification, protection of body, mind, and spirit. Thus, from the beginning, healing touch was not essentially a private moment but was shaped by the church's efforts to encourage wholeness and community in the midst of life's harsh realities." *Thomas, Zach. Healing Touch: The Church's Forgotten Language, p. 3–4*

"Our spiritual ancestors understood these truths intuitively. Most cultures regarded the heart as the seat of emotions, intellect, and will. The heart is cited symbolically throughout the Bible. Both the Hebrew Scriptures and the New Testament described the heart as part of the physical body, but it was also considered the point of contact with God. The heart as the inner point of human personality is open directly to God. It is said to be a place where God knew intimately the thoughts and emotions of the person, and the place where God could transform and Christ could dwell.

Most of Jesus' healings involved touch. This in itself was heretical and revolutionary, for he lived in a society of touching taboos. Social and religious rules rigorously defined what one could and could not touch. If one touched something or someone considered unclean, one became unclean oneself. Jesus broke all the taboos. He touched lepers and dead bodies. He responded to the touch of a menstruating woman. Regardless of how the community labeled him, he freely reached out to touch in love." *Graham, Litt, & Irwin. Healing From the Heart, pp. 21 & 34*

"The heart is a macrocosm of the universe – whatever is in your heart is everywhere. By knowing the mystery of your own heart, you begin to resonate with the mysteries of existence." *Sufi saying*

Directions for Using Healing Touch in Prayer

1. The person receiving Healing Touch sits in a chair and relaxes by breathing deeply and picturing a favorite meditative place.

2. A partner stands behind them, asks permission to touch and gently places their hands on the person's shoulder.

3. The partner or giver of Healing Touch takes a few minutes to become very centered within and to be present to the moment by letting go of all thoughts.

4. They then offer a prayer, asking to be a channel of God's love and compassion for the highest good of the person receiving Healing Touch.

5. Starting from the top of the head about four inches off the body, their hands do a raking motion slowly moving down to the feet. This is repeated all around the body until the area around the body feels clear of static or heaviness.

6. Next, they use their hands to fluff the energy around the body, using a light smoothing motion with one hand following the other. They end by returning to the starting position and silently offering a blessing to their partner.

7. The partners exchange places and repeat the process.

Guided Meditation #8

Opening the Heart

Allow the sound of the Tibetan Harmony Bowl to draw your attention inward to the place of peace and rest where God waits for you. (Ring the bowl)
Breathe deeply and feel your body releasing and totally resting. There is nothing to do, nothing to worry about; you need only to rest and to be restored.

Begin to feel a warm glow in the center of your heart and become aware of the small flame there that never goes out. As you gaze inwardly at the flame, watch it grow larger and larger. Feel the warmth begin to spread outward through your chest and torso, healing, loving and strengthening all the organs of your body. This loving energy from your heart continues to fill your arms, legs, and head until your whole being glows with radiance. Savor this experience until you feel the desire to send out this loving energy. Imagine it pouring from your heart, first to your family, friends, and community. Then image it filling your state, your country, and your continent. Finally, see the world surrounded by this radiance that continues to expand into the galaxy and universe.

As the sound of the ringing bowl draws you back to the awareness of this room, bring back with you the image and feeling of this loving energy from your heart filling all of God's creation. (Ring the bowl)

Give thanks for your ability to reach out with unconditional, loving energy and continue to feel the radiance of your own being.

Gathering

1. Welcome and arrange the altar.

2. Light the candle for a few minutes of silence and centering.

3. Ask the two questions:
   How are you in body/mind/spirit today?
   What has been your experience of God since we last met?

Presenting the Theme

1. Take turns reading the selections "To Dance with Life." Allow a pause between each one for individual reflection. (see p. 62)

Prayer

1. Play Guided Meditation #9.

2. Journal and draw, expressing the experience individually.

3. Share as a group what each person experienced.

4. Play "To Dance with Life" from the <u>Phenomenon</u> CD. Ask each person to express what they have learned or are feeling through free form movement, or groups of three to four people could create a dance together to share with the group.

Closing

1. Close in a circle by reading "Believers in Life," as a final blessing. (see p. 63)

New References
Clark, Karen Kaiser. <u>Life Is Change – Growth Is Optional</u>. Center for Executive Planning, 1993.
Ferry, Brian. "To Dance with Life." <u>Phenomenon</u> CD. Motion Picture Artwork, 1996.

To Dance with Life

"There is a vitality, a life force, an energy, a quickening, that is translated through you into action, and because there is only one of you in all time, this expression is unique. And if you block it, it will never exist through any other medium and will be lost." *Martha Graham*

"God does not ask anything else of you except that you let yourself go and let God be God in you." *Meister Eckhart*

Psalm 16: 5-9, 11
The Lord is my chosen portion and my cup; you hold my lot.
The boundary lines have fallen for me in pleasant places; I have a goodly heritage.
I bless the Lord who gives me counsel; in the night also my heart instructs me.
I keep the Lord always before me; because he is at my right hand, I shall not be moved.
Therefore my heart is glad, and my soul rejoices; my body also rests secure.
You show me the path of life.
In your presence there is fullness of joy; in your right hand are pleasures forevermore.

Matthew 5:16
Let your light shine before others, so that they may see
your good works and give glory to your Father in heaven.

"A life of prayer – or the spiritual life or the interior life, whatever term one uses for this journey that we have undertaken – is not completely linear, any more than one's intellectual or emotional life is linear. It is cyclical; it turns and turns and turns again, and carries us along with it.

It is that turning that caught my attention. It is that turning, that Dance, and its rhythms and steps and habits and joys and sorrows that draws me now. If we are to live lives that enable us to hear more clearly who we really are, then we will have to learn to move to a rhythm that is superior to the ones we have fashioned for ourselves. We will have to discover the rhythms of prayer and life that can be found in the steps of the Ancient Dance of the Ancient of Days.

Our lives must be shaped by the same rhythms that shaped the ancients, those who have gone before us. Only then will we be able to take up our places and join in the general Dance." *Adapted from* Living Prayer *by Robert Benson*

"I am a seed that God has planted in the space of Universal time.
Growing, allowing the presence of the Christ to rise up in me.
I begin to flower right where I am; under the order and direction of my creator.
The more I grow, the more I am, the more I have to give.
Rise up in me, oh God, create more of you in me."
Carolyn W. Darlington

Believers in Life

"The most masterful creators I know are those artists whose medium is life itself; life full of unfairness, unchosen seasons and seemingly impossible obstacles. Without hammer, clay or drum they neither pound nor impose. Their medium is being. Their presence adds beauty to the landscape of life.

In the face of misfortune they refuse to be diminished. In response to unfairness they become 'more' not less. Drawing on roots they themselves sometimes question, they continue to hope and to grow. Storms may whittle away their outer attractiveness and exhaust the strength of their spirit. However, over time those same storms only prove to be chisels that chip away at what conceals their raw courage and masks their real beauty.

In response to misfortune they continually find ways to recreate and to celebrate. Whatever their presence touches, increases life. From ashes they fan light alive. Awakening from shattered dreams they envision new horizons. In the silence of despair they hum soothing melodies. Washed anew and refreshed in their own fallen tears, they become wells of compassion for others.

These masterful creators weave memories, paint visions and sculpt beauty out of brokeness. They sing, laugh, love and cry. They work through their anger and learn to forgive. They listen to our Mother Earth and search to find their siblings. Creatively and courageously they risk to become who life challenges them to be. They are the artists of being alive, living treasures, True Believer's in Life. Oh, My Friend. I question if I would have seen this day, had not those creative examples helped me find my way. What gifts are my sisters and brothers!"

Clark, Karen Kaiser. Life is Change – Growth Is Optional, p. 91

Guided Meditation #9

To Dance with Life

Allow the sound of the Tibetan Harmony Bowl to draw your attention inward to the place of peace and rest where God waits for you. (Ring the bowl)

Breathe deeply and feel your body releasing all tension and totally resting. There is nothing for you to do, nothing to worry about; you need only to rest and to be restored. Image yourself as a lump of clay in the Hands of God. What color is the clay? What is the consistency? As God places you on the potter's wheel and begins to form you into a vessel, feel the love and tender care of His hands filling your being.

What is the form you are taking? Notice the details: the color, the shape, the design of the vessel you are becoming. What are God's intentions for you with what God is creating? Consider how this vessel is to be integrated into your life now. How will it assist you on your journey? How will it touch other's lives?

Thank God for creating you in such a wonderful form. At the ringing of the bowl, bring the image of your vessel and all its meaning back with you to the circle. (Ring the bowl)

Gathering

1. Welcome and arrange the altar.

2. Light the candle for a few minutes of silence and centering.

3. Ask the two questions:
   How are you in body/mind/spirit today?
   What has been your experience of God since we last met?

Presenting the Theme

1. Take turns reading the selections on "Sacred Time in the Celtic Tradition." (see p. 66)

2. Participants silently read "Timebound vs. Timeless Awareness" and "How Do You Metabolize Time?" and journal about how they experience time. (see pp. 67–68)

Prayer

1. Play Guided Meditation #10.

2. Share as a group what they experienced.

3. Listen to "Morning Has Broken" on the <u>Cat Stevens</u> CD.

Closing

1. Close in a circle by reading "Slow Me Down, Lord," by Wilfred Peterson, as a blessing. (see p. 69)

New References
<u>Cat Stevens Greatest Hits</u>. A&M Records Inc. 1983.
Chopra, Deepak. <u>Timeless Body, Timeless Mind</u>. New York: Harmony Books, 1993.

Sacred Time in the Celtic Tradition

"A fifth characteristic of Celtic spirituality has to do with their understanding of time. The early saints appreciated time as a sacred reality blessed and already redeemed by God's over-flowing compassion. This awareness of the sacred dimension to time is not the same as modern Western culture's frantic preoccupation in which 'every minute counts.' Rather, the Celts' perception was that there is a fullness now to all of time, manifest in the old Irish saying, 'When God made time, he made plenty of it.' With this perception of time as a gift from God, time in a chronological sense (with one historical event following another) was disregarded by the early Celts. For them, the present contains within itself both past events, which continue to live on, as well as the seeds of future events waiting to be born.

Without clear demarcations between past, present, and future, Celtic Christians interpreted history differently than we do. They made contemporaries of those who historically could never have been.

In many ways Celtic Christians saw the larger truths of myth and the lasting effect of rela-tionships of love standing outside of time, having an eternal quality that certainly cannot be understood fully by considering chronological time alone. The early Celts also believed in 'thin places'; geographical locations scattered throughout Ireland and the British Isles where a person experiences only a very thin divide between past, present, and future times; places where a person is somehow able, possibly only for a moment, to encounter a more ancient reality within present time; or places where perhaps only in a glance we are some-how transported into the future."

Sellner, Edward. Wisdom of the Celtic Saints, pp. 24–25

"The third characteristic of MacLeod's Celtic spirituality, or way of seeing, was his sense of the immediacy of the spiritual realm, of God's presence in the whole of life. It included a keen mystical awareness of those who have long gone before and the host of heaven present among us on earth. Iona he often described as "a thin place," in which the spiritual world is very close to the material." (Iona is an island off the coast of Scotland, where the first Celtic Abbey was built in the sixth century.)

Newell, Philip. Listening For The Heartbeat of God, p. 89

"A people who farmed and knew the pattern of the seasons, who lived close to the sea and watched the ebb and flow of tides, above all who watched the daily cycle of the sun and the changing path of the moon, brought all of this into their prayer. Here is a way of praying that is essentially holistic. I am reminded that as a human being living on this earth I am a part of the pattern of day and night, darkness and light, the waxing and waning of the moon, the rising and setting of the sun. The whole of my self is inserted into the rhythm of the elements and I can here learn something, if I am prepared to, of the ebb and flow of time and of life itself. The holding together of dark and light, cold and warmth, came natu-rally to a people whose whole livelihood showed death and rebirth, dying and new life, was a natural and inevitable part of their existence."

DeWaal, Esther. The Celtic Way of Prayer, p. 6

Time-Bound versus Timeless Awareness

Time-bound awareness defined by:

1. external goals (approval from others; material gain)

2. deadlines and time pressure

3. self image built up from past experiences

4. lessons learned from past hurts and failures

5. fear of change; fear of failure

6. distraction by past and future (worries, regrets, fantasies)

7. longing for security (never permanently achieved)

8. selfishness, limited point of view (what's in it for me?)

Timeless awareness defined by:

1. internal goals (happiness; self-acceptance; creativity; satisfaction that one is doing one's best at all times)

2. freedom from time pressure; sense that time is abundant and open-ended

3. little thought of self-image; action focused on the present moment

4. reliance on intuition and leaps of imagination

5. detachment from change and turmoil; no fear of death

6. positive experiences of being

7. selflessness; altruism; sense of shared humanity (can I help?)

8. sense of personal immortality

Chopra, Deepak. Ageless Body, Timeless Mind. pp. 292–293

How Do You Metabolize Time?

Read the following sentences and check off each one that applies to you fairly often or that you generally agree with. Even if you have seemingly opposed traits and opinions, answer each statement on its own. Part 1 represents chronos time. Part 2 represents kairos time.

Part 1

☐ There's barely enough time in the day to do all the things I have to do.
☐ I'm sometimes too exhausted at night to get to sleep.
☐ I've had to abandon several important goals I set for myself when I was younger.
☐ I'm less idealistic than I used to be.
☐ It bothers me to let unpaid bills sit around.
☐ I'm more cautious now about making new friends and entering serious relationships.
☐ I've learned a lot from the school of hard knocks.
☐ I could be a lot wiser about how I spend my money.
☐ I spend more time and attention on my career than on my friends and family.
☐ Life is a balance of losses and gains; I just try to have more gains than losses.
☐ In a loving relationship, the other person should be counted on to meet my needs.
☐ It sometimes hurts to remember the people I have let down.
☐ Being loved is one of the most important things I can think of.
☐ I don't like authority figures.
☐ For me, one of the most frightening prospects about old age is loneliness.

Part 2

☐ I do what I love, I love what I do.
☐ It's important to have a greater purpose in life than just family and career.
☐ I feel unique.
☐ Near-death experiences are very real.
☐ I often forget what day it is.
☐ I would describe myself as a carefree person.
☐ It's a good thing to bring sexual issues out in the open, even when they are disturbing.
☐ I work for myself.
☐ It doesn't bother me to miss reading the newspaper or hearing the news.
☐ I love myself.
☐ I've spent time in therapy and/or other self-development practices.
☐ I don't buy into everything about the New Age, but it intrigues me.
☐ I believe it is possible to know God.
☐ I am more leisurely about things than most people.
☐ I consider myself a spiritual person; this is an area of my life I work on.

Chopra, Deepak. *Ageless Body, Timeless Mind*. pp. 294–295

Slow Me Down, Lord

Ease the pounding of my heart by the quieting of my mind.

Steady my hurried pace with a vision of the eternal reach of time.

Give me, amid the confusion of my day, the calmness of the everlasting hills.

Break the tension of my nerves and muscles with the soothing music of the singing streams that live in my memory.

Help me to know the magical, restoring power of sleep.

Teach me the art of taking minute vacations:

Of slowing down to look at a flower,
to chat with a friend,
to pat a dog,
to read a few lines from a good book.

Remind me each day of the fable of the hare and the tortoise, that I may know that the race is not always to the swift – that there is more to life than increasing its speed.

Let me look upward into the branches of the towering oak and know that it grew great and strong because it grew slowly and well.

Slow me down, Lord, and inspire me to send my roots deep into the soil of life's enduring values that I may grow toward the stars of my greater destiny.

Wilfred Peterson

Guided Meditation #10

Sacred Time

Allow the sound of the Tibetan Harmony Bowl to draw your attention inward to the place of peace and rest where God waits for you. (Ring the bowl) Breathe deeply and feel your body releasing all tension and totally resting. There is nothing for you to do, nothing to worry about; you need only to rest and to be restored.

As you rest in this holy place, image a white light filling your body until it is radiant. See the light going out of the top of your head and surrounding your body. As the light continues to expand around you, notice how you begin to have a sense of merging with all of creation. Rest for a few moments in this timeless dimension of eternity.

You will now travel backward in time. Ask for a method of transportation and begin the journey back to a sacred moment in your life in the past. Carefully recall this experience and allow your senses to take in everything: the sounds, the sights, and the emotions you are feeling. Is someone there with you? Make this time fully alive and enjoy it. Bring back this moment from the past into the present.

Next, use your transportation to go forward to vision a sacred moment in the future. What are you seeing? Experience this fully: the feelings, the sights, the sounds, and the people that may be with you. Bring this moment from the future back to the present moment.

Feel the sacredness of the present moment enhanced by the past and the future. Notice the threads of connection. Allow the ringing of the bowl to draw your awareness back to the circle, carrying with you a deep sense of the fullness of time. (Ring the bowl)

Gathering

1. Welcome and arrange the altar.

2. Light the candle for a few minutes of silence and centering.

3. Ask the two questions:
   How are you in body/mind/spirit today?
   What has been your experience of God since we last met?

Presenting the Theme

1. Take turns reading "World Prayers." (see pp. 72–73)

Prayer

1. Play Guided Meditation #11 on Centering Prayer. (see Journey 2)

2. Journal and draw about your prayer experience.

3. Share as a group how it felt to experience Centering Prayer.

4. Read together "Signs of Inner Peace." (see p. 74)

5. Move the Tai Chi Five Elements to "From A Distance" on the Nancy Griffith CD.
(See Journey 4 for the movement explanation)

Closing

1. Close in a circle by reading "The Prayer of St. Francis of Assisi" as a blessing.
(see p. 75)

References

The Best of Nancy Griffith CD. Nashville: MCA, 2001.

Beversluis, Joel. A Sourcebook for the Community of Religions. Chicago: The Council for a Parliament of the World's Religions, 1993.

Rienstra, Marchiene. Swallow's Nest. Grand Rapids, MI: Eerdmans Publishing, 1992.

Roberts, Elizabeth and Amidon, Elias. Life Prayers. San Francisco: Harper, 1996.

World Prayers

A Baha'i Teaching from A Sourcebook for the Community of Religions

"When Love is realized and the ideal spiritual bonds unite the hearts of men, the whole human race will be uplifted, the world will continually grow more spiritual and radiant, and the happiness and tranquility of mankind be immeasurably increased. Warfare and strife will be uprooted, disagreement and dissension pass away, and Universal Peace unites the nations and peoples of the world. All mankind will dwell together as one family, blend as the waves of one sea, shine as stars of one firmament, and appear as fruits of the same tree. This is the happiness and felicity of humankind. This is the illumination of man, the glory eternal and life everlasting; this is the divine bestowal."

Psalm 108 – A Christian Reading

"With my heart fixed on You, O God, I will make glorious melody!
I will take up musical instruments and with singing awake the dawn!
I will thank You, El Shaddai, among all the peoples,
I will praise You among all the representatives of the nations.

For Your mercy is as high as the sky, and Your faithfulness reaches
to the clouds. Be exalted above the heavens, O God, and let your glory
fill the whole earth! Deliver Your beloved ones, and save me with
Your hand of love. Answer my prayer!

God speaks in Her holiness:
'I rejoice in the cultures of the earth's varied peoples.
I grant them the land they live on.
I claim many peoples as mine, to use for my saving purposes.
I will shout in triumph over those who fight against me and my will.'

Think about this: who can help us reach our goals if God rejects us?
She does not march forth with our armies.
Human help is vain if God's grace is absent from our struggles.
But with God, we can do great things.
It is She who will defeat all violence."

Rienstra, Marchiene Vroon. The Swallow's Nest

A Native American Reflection from Life Prayers, p. 251.

"I add my breath to your breath that our days may be long on the Earth, that the days of our people may be long, that we shall be as one person, that we may finish our road together." *Laguana Pueblo prayer*

A Jain Prayer from A Sourcebook for the Community of Religions, p. 237.

"Lead me from Death to Life, from Falsehood to Truth.
Lead me from Despair to Hope, from Fear to Trust.
Lead me from Hate to Love, from War to Peace.
Let Peace fill our heart, our World, our Universe."

A Buddhist Reflection from A Sourcebook for the Community of Religions

"Now under the loving kindness and care of the Buddha, each believer of religion in the world transcends the differences of religion, race and nationality, discards small differences and unites in oneness to discuss sincerely how to annihilate strife from the earth, how to reconstruct a world without arms, and how to build welfare and peace of mankind, so that never-ending light and happiness can be obtained for the world of the future. May the Lord Buddha give His loving kindness and blessing to us for the realization of our prayers."

A Hindu Reflection from Life Prayers, p. 44.

"O God, scatterer of ignorance and darkness, grant me your strength.
May all beings regard me with the eye of a friend, and I all beings.
With the eye of a friend may each single being regard all others."
Yojht Veda, XXXVL, 18

An Islamic Prayer from A Sourcebook for the Community of Religions

"Oh God, You are Peace.
From You comes Peace.
To You returns Peace.
Revive us with a salutation of Peace,
And lead us to your abode of Peace."

A Jewish Reflection from Life Prayers, p. 128.

"The threat to our salvation is the clash of peoples: Jews and Arabs, offspring of a single father, separated in youth by jealousy, in adolescence by fear, in adulthood by power, in old age by habit. It is time to break these habits of hate and create new habits: habits of the heart that will awake within us the ceaseless love of redemption and peace."
Rabbi Rami M. Shapiro

Namaste

I honor the place in you where God resides, which is of love, of truth, of light, and of peace. When you are in that place in you and I am in that place in me, we are one.

"Signs of Inner Peace"

1. An increasing ability to enjoy each moment

2. A tendency to act spontaneously rather than react to fear

3. A decreasing interest in judging others

4. A decreasing interest in judging oneself

5. An increasing preference to allow things to happen rather than to make things happen

6. A lessening inclination to interpret the actions of others

7. A decreasing involvement in conflict

8. An increasing ability to give and receive love

9. Less motivation to worry

10. Frequent, overwhelming periods of gratitude

11. Feelings of contentment and oneness with humanity and nature

12. Frequent attacks of smiling

13. Feelings of effervescent joy

Prayer of Saint Francis of Assisi

Lord, make me an instrument of Your peace.

Where there is hatred, let me sow love.

Where there is injury, pardon.

Where there is doubt, faith.

Where there is despair, hope.

Where there is darkness, light,

And where there is sadness, joy.

O Divine Master, grant that I may not so much seek

To be consoled, as to console;

To be understood, as to understand;

To be loved, as to love.

For it is in giving that we receive;

It is in pardoning that we are pardoned;

And it is in dying that we are born to eternal life.

Amen

Guided Meditation #11

Centering Prayer

Allow the sound of the Tibetan Harmony Bowl to draw your attention inward to the place of peace and rest where God waits for you. (Ring the bowl) Breathe deeply and feel your body releasing all tension and totally resting. There is nothing for you to do, nothing to worry about; you need only to rest and to be restored.

Feel a spaciousness within opening to receive God. Allow your mind to totally empty, except for one sacred word on which you focus. Experience God's presence without thoughts or images.

As you go deeper and deeper into the stillness, let go of distractions by returning to your sacred word. Feel the emptiness and silence grow as the peace of God fills and surrounds you.

Let the sound of the ringing of the bowl bring your awareness slowly back to the circle. (Ring the bowl) Savor the experience of centering prayer.

Gathering

1. Welcome and arrange the altar.

2. Light the candle for a few minutes of silence and centering.

3. Ask the two questions:
   How are you in body/mind/spirit today?
   What has been your experience of God since we last met?

Presenting the Theme

1. Take turns reading the selections on "Discernment." Allow a pause between each one for personal reflection. (see pp. 78–79)

2. Discuss the suggestions for "Discernment Tools." (see p. 79)

Prayer

1. Read through the Discernment Process adapted from "The Spiritual Exercises of St. Ignatius of Loyola." Ask group members to select a decision or issue in their lives that needs more clarity. Allow time for the participants to individually reflect on and write about sections I through IV. (see pp. 80–81)

2. Play Guided Meditation #12 to experience the discernment process.

3. Ask participants to return to the discernment sheet and finish section VI. The positive experiences from the meditation are listed under the + sign and the negative experiences are listed under the – sign. Privately pray section VII, the Election.

4. Bring the group back together and pray VIII, the Confirmation, together.

5. Offer individuals an opportunity to share their experiences of the discernment process.

Closing

1. Close with the blessing, "I am teachable and hold a beginner's heart," from <u>Blessings</u> by Julia Cameron, p. 174.

New References

Bergan, Jacquelini & Schwan, Marie. <u>Freedom, A Guide for Prayer</u>. Winona, MN: St. Mary's Press, 1988.
Ignatius of Loyola. <u>Spiritual Exercises and Selected Works</u>. George E. Ganss. New York: Paulist Press, 1991.
Lindbloom, Lois. "Hearing a Voice." <u>Presence: The Journal of Spiritual Directors International</u>. Vol. 5: 2.
May, Gerald. <u>Care of Mind, Care of Spirit</u>. San Francisco: Harper, 1992.
Nouwen, Henri. <u>The Inner Voice of Love</u>. New York: Doubleday, 1996.
Teresa of Avila. <u>The Interior Castle</u>. Tr. & Ed. Pl Allison Peers. New York: Image Books, 1989.

Discernment

2 Corinthians 3:17
"Where the spirit of the Lord is, there is freedom."

"Lived holiness is continually choosing to do that action which is here and now the best concrete act of love of God and other people. The Christian conscience must discern how best to live love in each complex situation of life."
Futrell, John Carroll. <u>The Still, Small Voice</u>

"To live a disciplined life is to live in such a way that you want only to be where God is with you. The more deeply you live your spiritual life, the easier it will be to discern the difference between living with God and living without God, and the easier it will be to move away from the places where God is no longer with you. You have your own inner knowledge to answer that question. Your will be done, not mine. Give every part of your heart and your time to God and let God tell you what to do, where to go, when and how to respond. God does not want you to destroy yourself. Exhaustion, burnout and depression are not signs that you are doing God's will. God is gentle and loving. God desires to give you a deep sense of safety in God's love. Once you have allowed yourself to experience that love fully, you will be better able to discern who you are being sent to in God's name." *Nouwen, Henri.* <u>The Inner Voice of Love</u>, *p. 23*

"May identifies hearing an inner voice as one of several examples of sensory experience with spiritual implications. It reveals an opening of human awareness at a level of consciousness not usually experienced. He describes the movement away from such awareness as willfulness – a movement that protects one's image of self, hangs onto familiar patterns of thought and resists opening and surrendering to Mystery. It is when attachment and willfulness are relaxed that willingness can provide a hospitable place for our desire for God and God's desire for us to be welcomed into awareness. It is the fruits of the experience that count: the impact the experience has upon one's life and love. Often the fruit cannot be assessed for some time after the event, but it is an essential criterion for evaluating a spiritual experience." *May, Gerald.* <u>Care of Mind, Care of Spirit</u>

Prayer of Father Mychal Judge, who lost his life on September 11, 2001 serving as chaplain to NY firefighters:

"Lord, take me where you want me to go;
let me meet who you want me to meet;
tell me what you want me to say,
and keep me out of your way."

Criteria for confirming that a message is from God, by Teresa of Avila, a sixteenth century mystic, in her book, <u>The Interior Castle</u>:

1. The message carries a sense of power and authority; in just a few words the person is comforted or directed.

2. It results in peace in the soul of the person, whose attention is drawn to recalling and praising God.

3. The words remain with the person for a long time, leaving an impression of the certainty of the message.

Summarized by Lois Lindbloom in "Hearing A Voice," in <u>Presence</u>

Discernment Tools

1. What resources can you draw on to help focus on the problem?

2. What support systems can you use for advice/support to hear yourself, to sort things out, or think out loud? (Soul friend)

3. From your perspective, are there any moral principles that you hold absolutely which impact your decision?

4. Is there harmony between your own feelings and other input?

5. Who would be affected by your decision or change?

6. Are you conscious of those affected as you move through this process?

7. What is your image of yourself during this experience?

8. What is your image of God during this experience?

9. What would lead to freedom of spirit to make an informed choice that takes the responsibility to co-create the future with God?

10. What would lead to more truth, compassion, and justice?

11. Is the decision rooted in the true self in relationship to God or in the false self that is wounded, needy or ego based?

12. Will the decision result in "Fruits of the Spirit": peace, joy, patience, love, generosity, and kindness?

13. Will the decision be life giving and lead to greater good and a deeper relationship with God?

14. Is it congruent with life circumstances, leading to harmony in all areas?

A Discernment Process

Adapted from the Spiritual Exercises of St. Ignatius of Loyola

It is essential for spiritual maturity to learn to make decisions that are in harmony with the spirit of goodness so that we are consciously shaping our lives to God's deepest desire and love for us. As we prayerfully discern the movement of Spirit within, it often becomes not just a choice between good and evil, but a movement from lesser good to greater good. The following process is an adapted form of "Decision Making in the Spirit" from <u>Freedom, A Guide for Prayer</u>, by Bergan and Schwan.

I. Preparation and call to love: As you begin this process, select a decision or issue in your life that needs more clarity. Ask for Divine presence to discover God's intent in regard to this decision or discernment.

II. Prayer: Gracious God, open my mind and heart to be attentive to all the ways you speak to me. Grant me the strength to turn within to spend time listening; give me wisdom to see your movement in my relationships and circumstances of my life; shine your light on my memories and emotions; remove obstacles or attachments that may block this process and give me courage to accept your guidance.

III. Gathering of evidence: May I be totally honest in discovering all the factors involved in this decision, my present commitments and condition of life, to see how they fit with the pattern of God's intention for my life.

IV. Prayerful reflection: Gracious God, bring into my awareness anything that will keep me from moving towards a deeper relationship with you and the fullness of this process. Make me aware of the patterns or dependencies that block my spiritual growth.

V. Prayerful reflection: Loving God, be present as I list the advantages and disadvantages of this decision. Heighten my feelings of harmony, peace, contentment, and inspiration that energize me (consolations). Guide me away from feelings of fear, anxiety, restlessness, discouragement, and alienation (desolations).

VI. Meditation: Play Guided Meditation #12. In your imagination, create a scenario of two possible decisions you could make regarding your issue, being aware of the movement of feelings and body sensations you experience with each one. Make notes below about the positive and negative aspects that are revealed to you in meditation.

+ consolations   − desolations

VII. Election: It is with a sincere heart that I have made this decision. Thank you for your presence and gift of love that sustains me. Grant me the courage to take action.

VIII. Confirmation: Faithful God, I pray that as I live into this decision, You will continue to guide me with feelings of peace and wholeness. May I always be mindful of you in the circumstances of my life and the unity of myself, others, and the Universe through you.

Guided Meditation #12

Discernment

As you deeply relax and image being filled with light, rest in the place of perfect peace within the center of your soul.

Become aware of a door that leads to a room where one of your choices is playing out in a scenario. Open the door and enter this scene. Notice all the details of what is happening. What is the mood? Who is there and what are they saying? Experience how you are feeling and how these feelings manifest in your body. Do you feel God's presence with you? Prepare to leave by completing anything that you feel needs to be done. Walk out, closing the door behind you.

As you leave the first room, you will see another door that will open to another of your options being demonstrated. Enter this room and experience fully what is happening. What is the mood? Who is there and what are they saying? Experience how you are feeling and how these feelings manifest in your body. Do you feel God's presence with you? Prepare to leave by completing anything that you feel needs to be done. Walk out, closing the door behind you.

When you are ready, slowly bring your awareness back to the circle. Bring back the impressions you have gathered from both rooms. Using this information, quietly write in section VI. Then pray section VII, the Election, to yourself.

Gathering

1. Welcome and arrange the altar.

2. Light the candle for a few minutes of silence and centering.

3. Ask the two questions:
   How are you in body/mind/spirit today?
   What has been your experience of God since we last met?

Presenting the Theme

1. Take turns reading the selections on "Gratitude." Allow a pause between each one for individual reflection. (see p. 84)

Prayer

1. Pray with the Philippians passage using Lectio Divina. (See Journey 2 for guidelines)

2. Journal and then draw what you experienced in prayer. Consider these questions: What are you grateful for? What are the blocks that keep you from fully feeling gratitude?

3. In pairs, share your prayer experiences and also name the blocks you wish to release so that you are free to feel gratitude more deeply.

4. Play "New Dawn" from The Mystic Harp CD as the partners take turns using the Healing Touch techniques taught in Journey 9.

5. Move the Five Elements of Tai Chi to "What A Wonderful World," on the Anne Murray CD.

Closing

1. Close by reading "A Prayer of Gratitude" as a blessing. (see pp. 85–86)

New References
Bell, Derek. The Mystic Harp CD. Clarity Sound and Light, 1996.
Murray, Anne. What A Wonderful World CD. Music Canada, 1999.
Rupp, Joyce. May I Have This Dance? Notre Dame: Ave Maria Press, 1992.

Gratitude

Philippians 4:6-9

Do not worry about anything, but in everything by prayer and supplication, with thanksgiving let your requests be known to God. And the peace of God, which surpasses all understanding, will guard your hearts and minds in Christ Jesus. Finally beloved, whatever is true, whatever is honorable, whatever is just, whatever is pure, whatever is pleasing, whatever is commendable, if there is anything worthy of praise, think about these things. Keep on doing the things that you have learned and received and heard and seen in me and the God of peace will be with you.

"It is only in proportion as we think of yesterday's supply that we sometimes run into lack; but as we learn to turn within for a fresh supply we draw forth God's grace in new forms, bigger forms, richer forms." *Joel Goldsmith*

"Giving thanks is an important state of your consciousness that keeps you in an awareness of oneness with Divine flow." *Eric Butterworth*

"Faith is a mental perception of what is good, together with a steady endeavor to live despite all obstacles. Keep your face to the sunshine and you cannot see the shadows." *Helen Keller*

"A hundred times a day I remind myself that my inner and outer life depends on the labors of other people, living and dead, and that I must exert myself in order to give in the measure as I have received and am still receiving." *Albert Einstein*

"Thank God, thank Him a million times over for those people, those rare, precious, marvelous people who have learned the secret place and pitched their tents there. Those who dwell in the attitudes of hope and confidence. Who reach across rather than down, those whose presence always leaves us feeling better about ourselves. Thank God for these loving people, these custodians of the secret of love." *Ernest Lanser*

Research on gratitude at University of California:

"Our research group wondered if an intentional grateful focus, practiced on a sustained basis, could have measurable beneficial effect on health and well-being. Compared to the hassles and events groups, participants in the gratitude groups felt more alive and energetic, and they were more optimistic concerning the upcoming week. They reported fewer physical complaints and spent more time exercising than did the subjects in the other two groups. Those in the gratitude group were also more likely to report helping someone with a personal problem or offering emotional support to another, suggesting that positive social behavior is a consequence of being grateful. Not only did they feel good, they also did good." *Emmons, Robert. Words of Gratitude*

A Prayer of Gratitude

(read responsively as a closing blessing)

"We are grateful   for eyes that can see and ponder.
for taste buds that know the sensuous pleasures
of eating and drinking.
for hands that hold and touch and feel,
for ears that can delight in music, and the voice of a friend,
for a nose that can smell the aroma of delicious food
and newly mown grass, and can also breathe the air that gives life.
We Thank You, God

We are grateful   for the treasures of loved ones whose hearts of openness
and acceptance have encouraged us to be who we are.
for the faithfulness of friends, walking with us when our
weaknesses stand out glaringly, delighting with us in our good
days and our joyful moments.
We Thank You, God

We are grateful   for the eyes of faith,
for believing in your presence which gives us hope in our darkest
days, encourages us to listen to our spirit's hunger, and reminds us
to trust in the blessings of your presence in our most empty days.
We Thank You, God

We are grateful   for the ongoing process of becoming who we are,
for the times of pain and growth,
for the great adventure of life that challenges and comforts us.
We Thank You, God

We are grateful   for your messengers, God – people, events, written or spoken
words – that came to us at just the right time and helped us grow.
We Thank You, God

We are grateful   that you call us to work with our multitude of gifts,
grateful that we can be of service and use our talents
in a responsible and just way.
We Thank You, God

We are grateful   that we have the basic necessities of life,
that we have the means and the ability to hear the cries of the
poor and respond with generous hearts.
We Thank You, God

We are grateful   for the miracle of life,
                            for the green of our earth,
                            for the amazing grace of our personal and national history.
We are grateful that we still have time to decide the fate of the world by our choices and actions, that we have it within our power to bring a divided world to peace.

                                      We Thank You, God

Faithful God, you have lavished us with love. Keep us ever mindful that you keep your promises. On our difficult days help us to remember that you are a refuge for those who need shelter, a comfort for those who feel empty and poor in spirit. On our joyful days fill us with a deep sense of thanksgiving as we experience your everlasting love. Help us to share your graciousness with all those who need a touch of tenderness."

Rupp, Joyce. May I have This Dance, p. 151

Gathering

1. Welcome and arrange the altar.

2. Light the candle for a few minutes of silence and centering.

3. Ask the two questions:
   How are you in body/mind/spirit today?
   What has been your experience of God since we last met?

Presenting the Theme

1. Take turns reading the selections about "Creativity." Allow a pause between each one for personal reflection. (see p. 88)

2. Explain the neurolinguistic process called "swish," that is adapted from Anthony Robbin's book, Unlimited Power. This process facilitates transformation by using the imagination to visualize a present behavior, or way of being, in the upper left hand corner of a large photographic negative image. Next, a smaller image of the desired behavior or way of being is placed in the lower right hand corner. Then using the idea of swishing through and changing something, the smaller image rapidly becomes brighter and larger as it moves through and changes the image on the left. This process is repeated several times with increasing speed.

Prayer

1. Play Guided Meditation #13, experiencing the "swish" process.

2. Ask participants to draw what they have experienced.

3. Play "State of Grace" from the State of Grace CD. Ask group members to create a movement that represents an old behavior or way of being, and a movement that represents a new, creative way of being. As they move back and forth between the two ways of being, they will be able to embody the new as they visualize what they wish to create in their lives. The old way of being will diminish and lose its power as the new takes over.

4. Return to the circle and present Wilferd Peterson's "Sacred Interpretation of the Scientific Approach to Creativity." (see p. 89)

Closing

1. Close by the group reading in unison "An Aramaic interpretation of the Lord's Prayer" as a blessing. (see p. 89)

New References

Aya, Jordan. Aha! New York: Three Rivers Press, 1997.

Fox, Matthew. Creativity: Where the Divine and the Human Meet. Tarcher/Putnam, 2002.

Peterson, Wilferd. The Art of Creative Thinking. Santa Monica: Hay House, 1991.

State of Grace CD. Windham Hill, 2002.

Creativity

Psalm 143:8
Teach me the way I should go, for to you I lift up my soul.

"A creative life increases understanding and appreciation of new ideas, of other people, and of the world in general. Creativity unlocks the mind and makes the spirit soar. In a word, creativity is what makes you feel alive." *Ayan, Jordan. Aha! p. 8*

"That which we give birth to from our depths is that which lives on after us. That which is inborn in us constitutes our most intimate moments – intimate with self, intimate with God the Creative Spirit, and intimate with others. To speak of creativity is to speak of profound intimacy. It is also to speak of our connecting to the Divine in us and of our bringing the Divine back to the community.

There is a river of creativity running through all things, all relationships, all beings, all corners and centers of this universe. We are here to join it, to get wet, to jump in, to ride these rapids, wild and sacred that they be." *Fox, Matthew. Creativity, pp. 2, 3 & 66, 67*

"In other words, every human faculty and sense in its truest form, every pure human affection and good desire for life is essentially an expression of God's life, God's voice, God's desire, and to enter deeply enough into these truly human characteristics is to approach the very mind and being of God. Again, the emphasis that comes across in Celtic spirituality and in this particular expression of it is that spirituality is not about looking away from life but more deeply into it, not about denying the human but about releasing our truest selves, and that the life of our truest self partakes of the very substance of God's life, the One Self that is at the heart of all selves." *Newell, Philip. Listening For the Heartbeat of God, p. 70*

"I believe that creativity is natural and innate. Creativity is part of our spiritual DNA. Just as we carry the blood that courses through our veins, we carry a primal need for self-expression. To my eye, creativity is as essential to human life as the urge to procreate or find shelter. When people access their creativity, they are accessing the divine power within them. As we open to this power, it fills our lives, and it brings with it spiritual health and abundance. We do become more beautiful, more clear, more focused, and more receptive to the divine flow as we open our hearts to a creative practice." *Julia Cameron*

"You were born with potential.
You were born with goodness and truth.
You were born with ideals and dreams.
You were born with greatness.
You were born with wings.
You're not meant for crawling, so don't.
You have wings.
Learn to use them and fly."
Rumi, Sufi mystic

"Sin is the refusal of the human to become who we are." *Rabbi Abraham Joshua Heschel*

Sacred Interpretation of the Scientific Approach to Creativity

1. Saturation, preparation, and stimulation: In your search for data, use the power of prayer. Ask to be directed to the people, the books, the facts you need.

2. Incubation: Once you have accumulated data and consciously worked on the problem, let go and let God. Release your problem to God with a prayer that the answer will come in its own time and place. Hold the attitude of faith and expectancy, knowing that God has all the answers, that God's knowledge is limitless and can never be exhausted.

3. Illumination: Keep your mind open. Have a quiet time each day to relax with an open mind, waiting for the ideas to come. When the inspiration comes, write your idea down in a notebook. Thank God for it and ask God to bless it and help you to put it to work to serve humankind.

4. Verification: Pray that you may judge ideas from the standpoint of truth and justice. Realize that only ideas in harmony with God's infinite laws of life are from Him. Evaluating ideas with the Golden Rule standard will eliminate those that are unworthy of your highest purpose.

Peterson, Wilferd. Adapted from The Art of Creative Thinking

An Aramaic Interpretation of the Lord's Prayer

O Cosmic Birther of all radiance and vibration!
Soften the ground of our being
and carve a space within us where your Presence can abide.

Fill us with your creativity so we may be
empowered to bear the fruit of your mission.
Let each of our actions bear fruit in accordance with our desire.

Endow us with the wisdom to produce and share
what each being needs to grow and flourish.

Untie the tangled threads of destiny that bind us,
as we release others from the entanglement of past mistakes.

Do not let us be seduced by that which would divert
us from our true purpose, but illuminate the opportunities of the
present moment.

For you are the ground and the fruitful vision, the birth, power
and fulfillment as all is gathered and made whole again.

Amen

Guided Meditation #13

Creativity

Allow the sound of the Tibetan Harmony Bowl to draw your attention inward to the place of peace and rest where God waits for you. (Ring the bowl) Breathe deeply and feel your body releasing all tension and totally resting. There is nothing for you to do, nothing to worry about; you need only to rest and to be restored.

Open your awareness to the gifts that God planted deeply within you at your birth. They are longing to emerge and you are being called to use them now in your life. Visualize the great person that God created you to be. What are you doing? How do you feel? Who is with you? Listen to the deep yearnings of your soul and hold them in the center of your being. They will help you to co-create your life with God.

Image a picture of yourself as you are now in the upper left corner of a large photographic negative. Fill in the details of your current life experience. Are you using your God given talents? Are you listening to the deep yearning of your soul? What is keeping you from fulfilling the call to become all that you can be?

Create a smaller image of your desired way of being in the lower right hand corner of the negative. Using a swishing motion, allow the smaller image to become brighter and larger as it moves rapidly up through the image on the left. Repeat this several times until the new way of being fills the picture. Experience the energy and power of how it feels to follow the calling of your soul.

Give thanks for and trust the Divine support and guidance that is with you as you move forward to co-create your life with God. Allow the sound of the bowl to bring your attention slowly back to the circle. (Ring the bowl)

"I have been part of the Footprints group since its inception. My expectation was that it was going to be a group of women who shared my desire to grow closer to God through the interaction of our different experiences, and this expectation continues to be fulfilled. I feel that I am being guided closer to God through methods other than just going to church. I like the variety of learning. I also think it takes an entire year to build up trust in the group; trust to really share your feelings and emotions.

I am a much calmer person today than I was two years ago. Little things don't bother me as much. My friends have noticed my different demeanor. When I was showing my spiritual/meditative garden to my friend Libby, she remarked, 'I'm telling you Suzy, you have really gotten weird but this garden is so cool! Can I use it too?'

I read daily devotionals. I certainly try to meditate every day, but because most of my spirituality draws from nature and the land, if the weather is bad, I don't get outside and I have yet to establish a spot inside that means as much to me as my meditative garden outside.

Life maps were most helpful. I feel this is a very important first step to get to know the people in your group. And this was the single most important thing I did for myself. It still hangs on my refrigerator as a daily reminder of who I am and why."

– **Suzy**

"I joined the group at the beginning when it was newly formed. The only expectation I had was that I hoped to be with a safe group of women who wanted to grow spiritually the same way I did.

I have experienced a warm bonding with some very special women. We have all dared to risk a little, expose ourselves a little, but it was always up to us, how much we wanted to contribute. There was never any pressure to share, just gentle nudging to grow each time we met.

From being in the group, I now try to meditate on a regular basis. I look for God in my daily life. I pray more often and I pray for others more often. I've learned how to turn things over to God and let them go more often.

I think the things that helped me most were the meditations, the sharing of stories of God working in our lives, and that there was always something new each week that we focused on. I also enjoyed the movement as a form of embodied prayer.

Whenever I left the group to go home, I always felt so relaxed and at great peace inside. My focus was brought back to God. I truly can't think of anything I would change about this special group. It has truly been a life changing experience for me."

– **Sue**

"Elizabeth Willey has developed a unique, spirit based method on integrating body, mind and soul. The Footprints method encourages each member to step into their awareness of God by experiencing various methods of spiritual prayer and connection. Our participants represented both conservative and liberal Christian backgrounds, yet all have found a common ground – a sanctuary of love, peace and acceptance.

I was able to attend only half the sessions, but I found in the sessions that I did attend, a growing sense of spiritual community and support. Members of our group were encouraged to bring their own contributions, and I was able to offer a New Year's burning bowl ceremony and a blessings workshop. Another member developed a unique and powerful meditation with watercolors. Footprints creates a space for each person to find personal empowerment and understanding. I am looking forward to this book as I intend to use it at my church to start a Footprints group using Elizabeth's methods and materials.

Footprints
We were on a path
Imprinted with the divine
Learning to walk on that path
And run on it
And leap
And stop
And turn around from time to time
And listen
And continue
Learning to dance on that path
And be blessed by its presence
Learning its spirals, up and down and around
Learning to balance
Learning to connect
Learning to be sad and glad
Learning to cry and let go
Learning to allow
Learning to trust
Learning to BE
Bless those footprints"
– Margo

"I wrote the following words four years ago and it seems even more relevant now in our spirituality group: We need to link lifeboats. Arm in arm, now in the greatest flood since Noah. We need to seek the solace and solutions by listening to Wordsworth's 'Still sad music of humanity.' We need to venture into Thoreau's woods 'to live deliberately.' We need to heed Christ's words according to Matthew and land our boats and build our houses 'upon a rock'...and when the floods come and the winds blow and beat upon that house it will fall not for it was founded upon a rock."

– **Penny**

"My initial thoughts in joining our Footprints group were curiosity, trust of our leader, a desire to be more spiritually connected, and to expand my awareness of the various tools and practices, ancient and evolving, for a soul-centered, healthy life. I wanted to be around others who share the same belief in holistic spirituality, healing, and growth in a loving, trusting environment. I hope to be able to take this personal growth of internal love to all the people I touch.

I have experienced a developing, growing depth and trust....a deepening connection with most of the women in the group and a care for the well-being of everyone. In the group itself, I have experienced a feeling of letting down, relaxing, being safe to express where I am today without the details of life...everybody has their stuff and this transcends it. It's like I'm okay with who I am on a whole different level...it's a soul level.

It has affected my daily life with growing awareness and use of the practices...realizing the presence of the Divine in everything I do is a big Aha for me! It really alters how I view things...mundane or otherwise. I have always felt gratitude, but now I feel gratitude with connection.

I love the clearing/centering in the beginning of our gatherings because it gets us right where we all need to be with ourselves and each other. And I love the movement like tai chi and painting and writing...all forms of free, unstructured self-expression. I like the interactive and group participation portions as well."

– **Susan**

"Prior to joining our 'Soul Circle,' I had been looking for a spiritual path, without really knowing that was what I was looking for. I had not had a good experience with Christianity and organized religion in general and was doing a lot of reading about Eastern philosophies. So I was very excited when Betsy asked me to join this group and felt that this was going to be a wonderful opportunity to explore further. I didn't know what to expect, but in my wildest dreams I could not have imagined all that have I received from being part of this journey with these incredible women.

My favorite journeys have been those that dealt with energy work, such as healing touch and tai chi. The guided meditations have helped me to develop a meditation practice at home and even though I know I could do more, I have also learned that I can only do what works for me - some days none of it fits, and on others it all comes together. I am continually amazed that whatever I seem to be needing on the day we get together, is somehow exactly what our journey is about that night. I feel like all of us have grown a tremendous amount and are not quite as reliant on Betsy to lead us. There have been times when one of us stepped in at the last minute to lead the group – something that I'm sure we would not have felt comfortable doing in the beginning.

The group has given me a sense of peace in my life that was never there before. That feeling comes from the guided meditations, the music and the movement. I have been able to include all of these in my daily life, making each day one to look forward to. The energy that comes to me from being with the group is amazing and that energy has carried into my everyday life. I can feel these friends with me always and I think it shows in my ability to get through the hard stuff. The power that comes from the group also helps me to believe that people working together in this way can effect change in the world."

– Julie

"I joined our group in the very beginning two years ago. I was very reticent about join-ing. I was nervous about someone trying to push me toward his or her beliefs. I didn't want to adopt someone else's beliefs, I was interested in enhancing my own journey and building on my own thoughts and ideas. I even thought about how I might quit the group gracefully without hurting anyone's feelings if I didn't like it.

As each new lesson was being explained, I always felt very skeptical about my ability to achieve and understand the different exercises. The little voice in my head whispered, 'you aren't centered or spiritual enough to arrive at any great conclusion through this method.' And I surprised myself every single time! I have learned new ways to think, make decisions and to LIVE more fully every single day. I am much more peaceful than I was when I began going to our Spiritual Group. I have lost that sense of 'aloneness' that I have always had. We have become a real source of strength, compassion and 'belonging' for each other. Together, we create a very powerful healing and peaceful place to gather.

We have learned such a variety of ways to achieve spirituality that everyone has been able to find what is best for them. Whether it is through music, movement, medita-tion, watercolors, prayer, nature or dreams, all of us take pieces of these to sew into our own experience, thoughts and ideas.

The most helpful lesson for me was the 'discernment' meditation. Funny enough, it was the one lesson I felt most confused about. I wasn't sure I understood the body/decision relationship. But I hung in and went through each step and followed instructions. I learned to listen to how my physical body felt under different circumstances. And like a ton of bricks it hit me! I was able to make a clear and complete decision about a nagging question I had had for a long time.

I wouldn't change a thing. I think every 2 weeks is perfect. And I look forward to learning more and more positive ways to look at, and live life."
– Chris

I needed a place to feel that I could experience a few moments of peace…and I needed to connect with the Divine Spirit within and learn to give up some of my control issues about needing to do everything myself. I hoped that I would find all of those. What I found was an acceptance of who I was…wherever I was…and wherever I was going. We were in different places spiritually, but that didn't matter.

There was an energy in the group that was purely divine spirit. We would do an exercise or meditate and I would feel the infusion of the energy from the room…and feel totally connected to everyone there even if I did not know them…and feel totally connected with everyone in the universe as well as the universal God spirit. It was awesome! We transcended the persons we were…we became one energy. There was no judgment… there was love and our God connection with each other.

I cherish the unconditional love and acceptance in our group."
– Linda Joy

Bibliography

Artress, Lauren. Walking A Sacred Path. New York: Berkley Publishing, 1995.

Aya, Jordan. Aha! New York: Three Rivers Press, 1997.

Barry, William. God And You. New Jersey: Paulist Press, 1987.

Bender, Sue. Plain and Simple. San Francisco: HarperCollins, 1989.

Bergan, Jacqueline and Schwan, S. Marie. Surrender. Saint Mary's Press, 1986.

Bergan, Jacqueline & Schwan, Marie. Freedom. Winona, MN: St. Mary's Press, 1988.

Beversluis, Joel. A Sourcebook for the Community of Religions. Chicago: The Council for a Parliament of the World's Religions, 1993.

Brandt, Leslie. Psalms Now. St. Louis: Concordia Publishing House, 1973.

*Cameron, Julia. Blessings. New York: Penguin Putnam Inc., 1998.

Carmichael, Alexander. Carmina Gadelica III. Scottish Academic Press, 1976.

Chopra, Deepak. Timeless Body, Timeless Mind. New York: Harmony Books, 1993.

Clark, Karen Kaiser. Life Is Change – Growth Is Optional. Center for Executive Planning, 1993.

de Mello, Anthony. Sadhana, A Way to God. New York: Doubleday, 1984.

*De Waal, Ester. The Celtic Way of Prayer. New York: Bantam Doubleday, 1997.

*Downey, Michael. Understanding Christian Spirituality. New Jersey: Paulist Press, 1997.

Farrell, Edward. Celtic Meditations. Denville, New Jersey: Dimension Books, 1976.

Foster, Richard. Celebration of Discipline Study Guide. San Francisco: HarperCollins, 1983.

Fox, Matthew. Creativity: Where the Divine and the Human Meet. Tarcher/Putnam, 2002.

Gendlin, Eugene. Focusing. New York: Everest House, 1978.

Graham, Litt & Irwin. Healing From the Heart. Canada: Wood Lake Books, 1998.

Hess, Herman. Siddhartha. New York: Bantam Books, 1951.

Ignatius of Loyola. Spiritual Exercises and Selected Works. George E. Ganss. New York: Paulist Press, 1991.

*Kaisch, Ken. Finding God. New Jersey: Paulist Press, 1994.

Kelly, Thomas. A Testament of Devotion. San Francisco: Harper Brothers, 1941.

Kisly, Lorraine. Ordinary Graces. New York: Bell Tower, 2000.

Lindbloom, Lois. "Hearing a Voice." Presence: The Journal of Spiritual Directors International. Vol. 5: 2.

May, Gerald G. Will and Spirit. San Francisco: HarperCollins, 1982.

May, Gerald. Care of Mind, Care of Spirit. San Francisco: HarperCollins, 1992.

Miller, Jean & Stiver, Irene. The Healing Connection. Boston: Beacon Press, 1997.

Mira, Mira & Shyam Mehta. Yoga The Iyengar Way. New York: Alfred A. Knopf, 1995.

Moore, Thomas. Care of the Soul. New York: HarperCollins,1992.

*Newell, Philip J. Listening For the Heartbeat of God. New York: Paulist Press, 1997.

Nouwen, Henri. The Inner Voice of Love. New York: Doubleday, 1996.

Nouwen, Henry. With Open Hands. Notre Dame, IN: Ave Maria Press, 1995.

O'Donohue, John. Anam Cara. New York: HarperCollins, 1997.

O'Donohue, John. Eternal Echoes. New York: HarperCollins, 1999.

Oldfield, David. The Adolescent Spiritual Journey. Washington, DC: The Foundation For Contemporary Mental Health, 1987.

Palmer, Parker. Let Your Life Speak. San Francisco: Jossey-Bass Inc., 2000.

Pearsall, Paul. The Heart's Code. New York: Broadway Books, 1998.

Pearson, Carol S. Awakening The Heroes Within. San Francisco: Harpercollins, 1991.

Peterson, Wilferd. The Art of Creative Thinking. Santa Monica: Hay House, 1991.

Rice, Howard L. A Book of Reformed Prayers. Louisville: Westminister John Knox Press, 1998.

Rienstra, Marchiene. Swallow's Nest. Grand Rapids, MI: Eerdmans Publishing, 1992.

Roberts, Elizabeth and Amidon, Elias. Life Prayers. San Francisco: HarperCollins, 1996.

Rupp, Joyce. May I Have This Dance? Notre Dame: Ave Maria Press, 1992.

Bibliography

Sellner, Edward. The Wisdom of the Celtic Saints. Notre Dame: Ave Maria Press, 1993.

*Smith, Linda. Called Into Healing. Colorado: HTSM Press, 2000.

Standish, N. Graham and Mc Cormack, Ellen. "A Foundational and Integrative Approach to Spiritual Direction." Presence: The Journal of Spiritual Directors International. Volume 7: no. 1 and 2.

St. Romain, Philip. Reflecting on The Serenity Prayer. Missouri: Liguori, 1997.

Teresa of Avila. The Interior Castle. Tr. & Ed. Pl Allison Peers. New York: Image Books, 1989.

Thomas, Zach. Healing Touch: The Church's Forgotten Language. Louisville: Westminister/John Knox Press, 1994.

*Thompson, Marjorie. Soul Feast. Louisville: Westminister John Knox Press, 1995.

Tucker, Lucy Abbott-Tucker. "Live Nearby, Visit Often. Focusing and the Spiritual Direction Process." Presence: The Journal of Spiritual Directors International. Vol. 7: 3.

*Ulanov, Ann & Barry. Primary Speech. Atlanta: John Knox Press, 1982.

Vest, Norvene. Still Listening. New Horizons in Spiritual Direction. Pennsylvania: Morehouse Publishing, 2000.

West, Melissa Gayle. Exploring the Labyrinth: A Guide for Healing and Spiritual Growth. New York: Berkley Publishing, 1995.

*Books recommended for leaders to read

Discography

Anne Murray. What A Wonderful World. EMI Music Canada, 1999.

Bell, Derek. The Mystic Harp CD. Clarity Sound and Light, 1996.

Burke, Susie. "Will You Come Home?" When October Comes CD. Rounder, 1991.

Cat Stevens Greatest Hits. A&M Records Inc., 1983.

Douglas, Bill. "Deep Peace." Celtic Twilight CD. San Francisco: Hearts of Space, 1994.

Enya Watermark CD. New York: Reprise Records, a Time Warner Co., 1988.

Josh Groban CD: Reprise Records, 2001.

Lion King CD: Walt Disney Records, 1994.

Shulman, Richard. Transformation at Assisi CD. Rich Heart Music, 1992.

State of Grace CD. Windham Hill, 2002.

Taize Alleluia CD. Chicago. GIA Publications, 1988.

The Best of Nancy Griffith CD. Nashville: MCA, 2001.

The Pilgrim CD. Dublin: Tara Music Co. Ltd., 1994.

Notes

About the Author

Elizabeth Wood Willey is a teacher, spiritual director, and certified Healing Touch practitioner. She graduated from the University of Michigan in 1968, majoring in English and History, and completed a two year internship in Spiritual Direction in 1998 at the Dominican Center in Grand Rapids, Michigan. She teaches a leadership class to high school students, leads spiritual journey groups, and facilitates retreats and classes for youth and adults related to the deepening of the spiritual life.

Elizabeth feels most at home in the beauty of God's wilderness, and has led trips for youth and adults to the Boundary Waters of Minnesota for the past 14 years. She grew up in the Congregational Church, attends a Methodist Church, and now finds her spirituality deeply expressed through Celtic Christianity. Her theology is both ecumenical and interfaith. Footprints of the Soul, A Creative Guide for Spiritual Journey Groups and Individuals, is a compilation of her experiences in teaching and spiritual direction.

She and her husband have three grown children and are now enjoying their new role as grandparents.

About the Artist

Christine Collins Woomer was given her first box of watercolors when she was five, and she hasn't stopped painting since. She graduated with a Bachelor of Fine Arts degree from Michigan State University. Her drawings, prints and paintings have been shown in galleries and are in private collections throughout the country.

Christine has illustrated two children's books, The Outdoor Museum, the Magic of Michigan's Marshall M. Fredericks, published by Wayne State University Press in 2001, and The Story of Trapper, a Friend for Life, published by Paws With a Cause in 2002, which she co-authored as well.

For information about the book, the author or a schedule of
Leader Workshops, go to the web site, **www.footprintsofthesoul.com**.

To order the book, call 1-800-247-6553
or go to www.atlasbooks.com/marktple/00992.htm

The CD was recorded by Rabbit Ear Productions in Grand Rapids, Michigan.
Contact Gene Parker at 616-866-2672

A portion of the proceeds from Footprints of the Soul will be donated to
MacKenzie's Animal Sanctuary. www.petfinders.org/shelters/mil33.html